SUAKIN

a

SUAKIN, 1885

BEING A SKETCH OF THE CAMPAIGN
OF THIS YEAR

BY

AN OFFICER WHO WAS THERE

LONDON
KEGAN PAUL, TRENCH & CO., 1, PATERNOSTER SQUARE
1885

PREFACE.

THE following chapters were written to
while away many hours of pain and suffering, and for the amusement of some
few friends.

They contain a simple record of the
events which made up a war of peculiar
privations and dangers, due to the climate
we toiled in and the foe we fought against.

Every statement made may be taken as
fact, and the experiences are those of one
who took part in the campaign — the
author.

No literary merit is claimed for the
story, such as it is, and the indulgence of
critics is therefore asked on behalf of one
who has carried a sword more often than
a pen.

CONTENTS.

SUAKIN, 1885.

CHAPTER I.

THE VOYAGE OUT.

In the dark days towards the end of January
news reached England telling us the exertions
of our soldiers on the Nile had been rendered
fruitless by treachery at Khartoum. For several
days the most conflicting accounts were received
as to the real state of affairs. At one moment
Gordon was said to have escaped the general
massacre and to have retired towards the
equator, at another that he was defending himself in a church; and then later on that he
had fallen—

> " His front with wounds unnumbered riven,
> His back to earth, his face to heaven."

Few will ever forget those days; a dull sense

B

of pain was felt by all as the cry was raised throughout the length and breadth of the land—Too late!

In spite of all the months of toil, and all the hardships and privations connected with Lord Wolseley's advance up the Nile ; in spite of the hazardous march from Korti to Metemmeh and the shedding of some of England's best blood, a fragment of the expedition had only sighted the walls of Khartoum to find that treachery had been beforehand, and that one of England's greatest heroes had fallen when succour was almost within reach. But this was no time for inaction, the *raison d'être* of the Nile expedition was no more, the power of the Mahdi was enhanced, and the fall of Khartoum had brought thousands of recruits to his standards.

A perpetual succession of cabinet councils, the closing of the telegraph wires for all messages except those from the government to Lord Wolseley for two or three days, and then the decision was promulgated that a fresh expedition was to be despatched immediately to operate from Suakin.

There was no doubt about the feeling of the country at this time. We had been too late, it was true, but we must strike afresh now, strike with an irresistible force, and quell once and for all the power of the fanatic and the false prophet in the Sûdan. It was no time now for further vacillation. The people of England demanded action; prompt, energetic, decisive. The cost was not to be counted; cost what it might a blow in real earnest was to be struck this time, and the power of the Mahdi crushed out for ever.

For a period of a fortnight there was a hurry and a bustle in all the war departments. Hundreds of fresh hands were taken on at Woolwich, and a scene of activity took place in the yards there such as has not been witnessed since the days of the Crimea.

In a few days the details of the new expedition appeared in the press, a number of vessels were immediately chartered for conveying this force to the scene of operations; and orders were sent out to India and Egypt for the immediate purchase of a large number of camels, mules, and horses, for the use of the Transport. A week followed during which the various portions of the force were inspected by H.R.H. the Commander-in-chief, and then every day a constant succession of transports left the shores of England, carrying a force more perfectly equipped in every detail than ever force was before.

On the evening of the 11th of February I was on my way home from the club, where I had been talking to various friends about the all-absorbing topic of the day. I was walking along the streets thinking what lucky fellows they were who were sailing the following week, and wishing, like every other soldier, that I could get a place somehow or other. I had reached my door when my reveries were interrupted by a telegraph-boy saying—

" Is this for you, sir ? "

Quite unsuspicious of what it contained, telegrams in these days being pretty well as plentiful as letters, I was somewhat astonished when I found the purport of the message was as follows :—

" From the Adjutant-General.—Be so good as to hold yourself in readiness to proceed to Suakin at once, and report yourself here the first thing to-morrow morning."

Had it not been to save the feelings of my wife, and otherwise alarming the household, I should have relieved myself by a good cheer ; as it was, however, I kept my feelings to myself, and commenced at once to put my affairs in order, and to make out a list of things I should require, and which were to be purchased the following day.

The next morning early found me in Pall Mall, reporting myself.

" Yes," said my interviewer, " you must proceed to Ireland at once, and fetch over some men from there in time to sail from Southampton on Tuesday next."

I must confess that, in spite of all my military ardour, this was rather a blow. To be ordered out was one thing, but to be started off to Ireland at two hours' notice, without a particle of kit belonging to me, was quite another pair of shoes. Putting on my pleasantest manner, therefore, and giving my assurance that I was perfectly ready to go anywhere I was ordered, I finished up by suggesting mildly that, being a married man with encumbrances, it was just a trifle inconvenient.

" Well," said Sir ——, " we will see if we can manage it. Sit down a moment."

In a few minutes my destination was, I am thankful to say, changed for Aldershot, and I went down there the same afternoon to ask for a couple of days' leave.

Monday, 16th of February, found me again at

Aldershot, and the next morning at an early hour, and in drenching rain, we marched to the station *en route* for Southampton. We were all on board Transport No. 7 by one o'clock, and by three o'clock that afternoon were clearing our decks of visitors and saying good-bye to many friends, while bands played and crowds cheered again and again on the wharf. It is always an impressive sight watching troops embark for active service, but one thing there is no doubt about—it is worse for those that are left behind on the shore than for those in the ship.

The next morning we were out of sight of Old England, and getting into what seemed like dirty weather ; and so it turned out, for in a few hours our ship was kicking her heels very freely, and many of us were feeling not quite the men we did twenty-four hours before. The Bay of Biscay kept up its old character, and we got severely knocked about. The men were in a miserable condition, and the troop decks were swamped with water and littered with every conceivable article to be found in a soldier's kit. I always find it very difficult to rise to the occasion at sea. "A life on the ocean wave" seems a horrible fate. This time proved no exception to the rule, and like many others on board, I spent two days in my bunk on a little ship's biscuit.

Sunday afternoon brought us to " Gib.," which was looking very beautiful and very grand, as it always does. We were not long in getting on shore, and as we were to stop for four hours to take some gunners on board, we made up a party and drove down into the town to luncheon at the " Royal." " Gib." was looking its best ; there had been plenty of rain, so wild flowers of all sorts abounded. After a luncheon, such as we had not eaten since leaving England, we took a walk round the North Front, and out to the neutral ground. There are few more imposing views than the Old Rock presents from the neutral ground. There is a wonderful air of majesty and strength about the place, and England will lose one of her brightest jewels when Gibraltar ceases to be her property. It *is* a place to be proud of, and there are few inches of it that are not familiar to me, as I was there more than five years one time. It was dark before we put to sea again, and as we rounded Europa Point a band was playing " Auld Lang Syne," and we could hear away in the darkness the sounds of cheering coming to us across the still waters of the Mediterranean. The next morning found us

pitching and tossing about merrily in a heavy
sea, with a magnificent view of the Sierra
Nevada on our port quarter, the snow-clad
peaks standing high up in the sky and gleaming
brightly in the warm sunshine. It is almost
always rough in this part of the Mediterranean,
and a severe tossing is, as a rule, experienced
until Cape Gata is rounded, when the wind and
sea often drop suddenly. We were very unfortunate on this occasion as, by the afternoon, we
were only doing four knots instead of thirteen
or fourteen, our usual pace. The sea was dead
ahead and broke clear over us from stem to
stern. The destruction of crockery must have
been considerable, the noise was almost indescribable ; it was as if we were a big tin box full
of pieces of china which some big giant had
picked up and shaken to his heart's content.
Soon after this we ran into lovely weather, the
sun shone bright and warm, and the sea danced
past us with its waves of deep sapphire hue.
It was now time to set to work, for we had much
to do in the next fortnight. The men had all
to be fitted with their kharkee kit and served
out with their cholera belts, goggles, spine-pro-
tectors, and veils. It certainly seemed as if the
people at home had determined no pains should

be spared to protect the soldier against the climate and the sun, although we on our side felt bound to confess that when we appeared in full battle array we resembled a number of perambulating Christmas-trees more than anything else.

We were also anxious to get the men to a little position drill, for many among them were young hands and had much to learn. Among my own men I found many who knew nothing whatever about a rifle, and many more who had never fired a shot ; so, explaining to them that their own safety, to say nothing of my own, lay in their being able to use their rifles with effect, we started to work in real earnest and two parades a day of an hour and a half each was the order. But it was not to be all work and no play on board, for we were all intent upon having a merry voyage and enjoying ourselves while we could. A list was opened for a series of athletic sports, and in a short time the entries showed that we should have many an afternoon's occupation. The events were as follows :—Long jump standing, wheelbarrow race, tug of war, Chinese puzzle, and cock-fighting, and much amusement was derived every afternoon by carrying out the programme. But we were

going to have evening entertainments besides
this, and many of us were hard at work getting
up a concert. Wherever there are soldiers you
may depend upon it you will have music—music
of a sort certainly, and not quite of a "Monday
pop" order, but still music which gives a great
deal of pleasure, and a great deal of amusement,
and is not altogether without a little sentiment
and pathos sometimes.

By good luck we had among the officers two
excellent pianists, and several performers on
the mandolin, banjo, accordion, and penny
whistle ; we also had one of the best performers
on the bones it was ever my lot to hear. To
fall back on, we had also in the company a
professional dancer and a professional clown,
also a conjuror ; so we were a merry family all
round.

Our days were taken up, then, as follows, and
one was pretty much like another. Réveille
sounded at six, then came breakfast at eight,
prayers at nine, when the whole company were
marched aft and at the word "caps off" the
clergyman began reading a psalm followed by
a few prayers, and finishing with the one for us
soldiers. There was always something impressive
to me in this service ; it only lasted ten minutes,

but every one was very attentive and all seemed
to join in it. Prayers over, there came the first
parade at 9.30, then dinners at twelve o'clock,
and parade again at 1.45. At 3.30 we were
running off the heats in the various athletic
events till five o'clock, when "retreat" sounded
and hammocks were drawn; the men also had
their evening meal, but we did not have our
dinner till 6.30. At 7.45, the piano having been
carried on deck, music followed, till "First Post"
sounded at 8.30 p.m., "Last Post" half an hour
later, and "Lights out!" at 9.15. So ended
the ordinary day's routine at sea.

But I must go back a little. The next land
we sighted was the Galita Islands, which are
sadly in want of a lighthouse. These islands
belong to Italy, and though the Government
would be glad to erect a lighthouse there,
people refuse to live on these islands, as they
are said to be haunted—at least so runs the
story.

On the 26th of February we saw Cape Bonn,
on the African coast, far away on our starboard
beam, and about midday we passed quite close
to Pantalaria, a very fine-looking place, and used
by the Italians as a convict station.

At 9.30 p.m. on the same day we passed

Gozo, and at 10 p.m. we sighted Valetta lights. After this we saw no land till we reached Port Said at 4 a.m. on the 2nd of March. Meanwhile our concerts were in full swing. The officers began by giving one to the men, the programme consisting of two piano solos, a comic song or so, two vocal duets, and a reading. The following night the men returned the compliment by giving a concert to the officers, and most amusing it was. A private soldier took command of the piano, and, defying any interference on the part of the singer, continued to bang out an accompaniment sometimes at the top of the piano and sometimes at the bottom, but always alike utterly and hopelessly independent of time and key. However, every one appeared very well satisfied, and the pianist above all. There was one man, a sergeant in the A.H.C., who had a really beautiful voice, a high tenor and well trained. He only knew two songs by heart, but these were both very good, and he took the precaution to have as his accompanist the accordion-player. The refrain of the most effective of his songs was one pointing out the uncertainties of life, and finishing with the words—

"What is coming, who can tell?"

This was encored again and again. The only other song with a certain sadness in it was sung by a trumpeter boy not more than fifteen years of age. He stood up a little nervously before the audience and sang a song the name of which I never heard, but the verses finished with—

> " It's only a leaf in my Bible,
> I picked from my poor mother's grave. "

He used to sing this song very frequently, as the men seemed fond of it, but I always noticed there was a certain quietness when it was over, though not from want of appreciation. There were many other well-known songs, and one of the most popular was that old friend the chorus of which runs—

> " Wrap me up in my old stable-jacket,
> And say a poor buffer lies low,
> And six stalwart comrades shall carry me
> With steps solemn, silent, and slow. "

It is always a mystery where the things come from, but soldiers never seem at a loss if anything is required, never mind what it may be. In this way, and to our utter astonishment, the professional clown appeared rigged up in a complete fancy kit, with a wig, a very large false nose and spectacles, and a " billycock " hat.

Some excellent step-dancing followed, and then
hats off and "God save the Queen," which was
never omitted.

Our musical talents were further turned to
account, and a choir having been formed, we
managed to chant the whole service on Sundays,
both morning and evening, very creditably.
The dawn was just breaking as we dropped
anchor at Port Said, and as we were to go
through the disagreeable proceeding of coaling,
every one who could get ashore did so directly
after breakfast. The town lies on a dead level
scarcely two feet above the water, and as far as
the eye can reach is one endless extent of sand
as flat as a billiard-table. We found some good
ship-chandlers, where we bought sundry provisions at a price, also one or two shops of the
Bon Marché order, where one could obtain anything, from a tea-tray to a double-barrelled gun,
or from a Bath bun to a complete suit of
Chinese armour. Port Said has, however, been
described over and over again, no doubt, so it is
not worth while wasting many words on it here.
By 11.30 a.m. we were all on board, and shortly
afterwards we started to wend our weary way
along the canal to Suez. I say "weary way"
because this is a very wearisome journey. The

speed is limited to five miles an hour, and setting aside constant stoppages, the risk of running aground, and the compulsory halts for the night after 6 p.m., there is nothing to relieve the monotony of the surrounding scenery. The canal is hemmed in by banks on each side, and as these are in many places high, a sense of breathlessness and suffocation is experienced. We were very unfortunate, as we had only reached the first Gare, some seven miles from Port Said, when the vessel in front of us went aground, and in spite of much tugging and hauling could not be got off again. There was nothing for it then but to make the best of it, so, having made fast to the banks, we took our men ashore in squads of twenty and practised them firing at some extemporized targets in the shape of old biscuit-boxes. This kept us employed till dark, when we returned on board hoping for better luck next day. There are some curious anomalies regarding the navigation of the canal. If a ship goes aground those behind it must stop too, though there is often plenty of room to pass. If demurrage is claimed by the owners of the vessels thus delayed the sum realized goes to the Canal Company. Again, the company compel every vessel to take one of their pilots ;

but if a vessel happens to go aground the pilot
is not to blame, and moreover the damage that
may be done to the banks of the canal by his
running the ship ashore is at once claimed
against the owners of the vessel. The cost of
going through the canal is nine shillings per
ton, and a further charge of nine shillings a head
for every one on board except the working
hands. Our ship, therefore, cost the sum of
£1823. This will give some idea of what it
must cost the country to send this expedition
through the canal. It must be a nice little
item in the total expenditure when the number
of ships and number of men are taken into consideration.

The first point of any interest after leaving
Port Said is the Lake Menzalah, or ancient
Serbonian Bog, where the great plague of
the fifth century B.C., which afterwards deso-
lated Athens, originated, and from which too
almost all the plagues which swept over Asia
Minor and across Europe in the Middle Ages
are supposed to have had their origin. The
shores of the lake, as well as its shallow
waters, are almost always covered with thousands upon thousands of flamingoes, standing
all exactly in the same position and in lines

fully three quarters of a mile in length. Ten miles further on you pass the Gare of El Kantara, through which runs the direct road from Cairo to Jerusalem. There are a few reed and mud huts adjoining the ferry, and it was here we saw the first of our future friends—a camel. We dragged along slowly and lazily in the burning sunshine, for the weather had now become very hot, and we had quite given up work in the middle of the day, our parades being early and late. The rest of the time was employed studying maps and books on the Sûdan. We had each been served out with four or five maps of Suakin and its surroundings, also of the route to Berber. These were all printed on white calico. We had also each a small English-Arabic Vocabulary, and a " Report on the Egyptian Provinces of the Sûdan, Red Sea, and Equator " issued by the Intelligence Department. The Arabic Vocabulary was the cause of endless amusement, and shouts of laughter were to be heard over the catechisms that went on and the efforts at pronouncing some of the most unpronounceable words.

Just before sunset we arrived at Lake Timsah, and got a sight of Ismailyeh. We did not stop here, but proceeded through the lake and into the canal again, where we anchored for the night between high banks and in a suffocating atmosphere. The next morning, by seven a.m., we were entering the Bitter Lakes, or Waters of Marah, and glad we were to get into this wide expanse of water, as we were able to quicken our pace a bit. We had a fine view of the mountains Gebel Geneffe, which run down the western side of the lakes, and about five miles inland. It must be twenty miles or more through these lakes, and then you enter the last section of the canal again, and before long sight the Mountain of Deliverance, or Gebel Attaka, at the foot of which stands the town of Suez. It is at the base of this mountain that the Israelites are supposed to have crossed the Red Sea. We were out of the canal by three p.m., and at anchor in Suez harbour before four o'clock (4th March). The port or harbour of Suez is connected with the town by a narrow isthmus about two miles in length, and along which runs the railway. A large open space adjoining the main wharf had been turned into a depôt for the camels, which had been collected from all parts of Egypt, and brought there to be branded with the Broad Arrow preparatory to being forwarded on to Suakin. There were about two thousand or more of these animals, and a great number had been already sent on.

We had no time to go ashore, and only just managed to get our first letters from England before we were off again. While we were in harbour three other transports came in, and as we steamed out again about seven o'clock, the troops on board these cheered lustily, rockets were sent up, blue lights burnt, and trumpets and bugles sounded the " Advance " and the " Charge." Of course we cheered back again till we were all as hoarse as crows.

We had been the first ship to leave England, and were very keen to be the first to arrive at Suakin; so our disappointment may be imagined when we suddenly discovered that we were going dead slow, and that something was wrong with our boilers. By the next morning these were repaired, and though we had lost a good bit of our start, we were still ahead of the other transports. We all began to feel the heat very much, and what little wind there was happened to be right behind us, so we regularly panted for breath in the middle of the day. Going down the Gulf of Suez, we had the coast in view the whole while. It is a fine, rugged outline, but

the mountains looked utterly bare and barren,
and there did not appear to be a particle of
vegetation anywhere. The next day was rough,
but the wind still behind us. It always is more
or less rough in the Red Sea, and there is almost
sure to be a strong wind blowing either up or
down it. I know this time the sea was quite
high enough to make some of us feel very uncomfortable. We had lost sight of the coast
since leaving the Gulf of Suez, but as the sun
went down in a mist on the evening of the 6th
of March, there stood up against it the sharp
peak of some great mountain, and then we
knew that the end of our journey was approaching, and that the next morning would see us
saying good-bye to the comforts of board ship
life, for we should be off Suakin.

CHAPTER II.

SUAKIN.

(*Lat.* 19° 17′ *N., Long.* 37° 20′ *E.*)

THERE are three different passages through the reefs leading to Suakin. The northern passage is the shortest route for vessels coming from Suez, but it is the most dangerous of the three, and ninety miles in length. The southern passage is of course the most direct route for vessels from India, and is somewhat shorter, being only sixty miles long. The easiest and shortest in point of mere distance is the middle passage, thirty miles long, and running almost due east and west. It was by this last-named passage that we entered, our captain being, like most other people, strange to the place. It was a very hot morning, and the air was thick with a hot haze, so that we did not sight the land until we were getting quite close to it. Then

miles and miles of desert, and a lofty and rugged
range of mountains in the distance suddenly
came into view.   As we approached nearer, we
could see, about four miles away on our right,
two camps ; these turned out to be the 49th
(Berkshire) and 70th (East Surrey). On the
left of the town of Suakin was another and
much larger camp, where a part of the Indian
contingent were lying. The whole country
looked a burnt, parched-up wilderness, without a
particle of vegetation except the dried-up bush
of the desert.   It certainly looked the hottest
place I had ever seen, with a sky like one great
sheet of burnished brass over head, and with the
sun scorching down on an arid waste of sand.

It was midday before we entered the long
narrow channel leading into the harbour.   The
navigation of this channel is very hazardous, as
it is nowhere more than 300 yards broad, and in
some places much less than this.   On both sides
run the low coral reefs, and woe betide the ship
that happens to run on them.   This channel,
which is fully three quarters of a mile in length,
opens into a lagoon or bay, in which are two
islands.   One of these is known by us as
Quarantine Island, and has been used all through
the war as a depôt, where stores were landed,

and as a starting-point for the railway. Several piers and landing-stages have been erected here by the Royal Engineers, and vessels of 4000 tons are able to moor alongside these and discharge their cargoes. On the second island stands the old town of Suakin, and connected with the mainland by a causeway built by General Gordon some years ago. The town proper, or old town, consists of a number of low, flat-topped houses of the ordinary Eastern type, built right up to the water's edge. The thoroughfares or streets are of deep sand, there being no necessity for roads, as wheel traffic is unknown here. On the mainland, and adjoining the causeway just referred to, is a suburb which has outgrown the town both in population and importance. Here there are several mosques and buildings of some pretensions, as well as a large open barrack occupied by a battalion of Egyptian troops. Beyond this again comes the native town, composed of a great number of huts made of a sort of coarse grass matting spread over a framework of stout sticks in several thicknesses. Outside all are the earthworks and defences, running completely round and enclosing the whole place; they have been all erected since 1881, as before this date the town was quite open. These defences are exceedingly strong, and of considerable extent, and stretch over a distance of nearly two miles. The greater part of the lines are composed of strong earthworks, but in parts high walls of coral have been built. The principal forts and redoubts in these lines, commencing from the right or western side of the town, are Gerzireh Redoubt, close to the edge of the lagoons, and connected by a wet ditch with Yamin Redoubt on its left. The lines here turn sharply to the southward, the next strong points being Lausari Redoubt, Oorban Redoubt, Wastanieh Redoubt, and Forts Carysfort and Euryalus, the strongest points of the whole of the defences. A little to the south-east of these two forts are Fort Commodore and Gedeedeh Redoubt, where the lines trend eastward till they reach the lagoons on the south side of the old town, passing through Fort Turk, and the Arab and Sphink Redoubts to the Left Redoubt. Outside these lines, and about three quarters of a mile distant, there is a complete chain of small, circular redoubts with the Right and Left Water Forts on the west, and Fort Foulah on the south.

There are two principal entrances in the lines on the right of Fort Carysfort, and at Yamin

Redoubt, this last being the one most used by us during the campaign.

There is a certain amount of trade carried on between Suakin and Suez, but this is much impeded by the heavy duties levied by the Egyptian Government.

Suakin has been formed by nature as the principal port of the Egyptian Sûdan and the Nile provinces, but has never risen to a position of any pretension, and even now its prosperity is only comparative. The place was formerly held directly subject to Turkey, but in 1865 it was sold and handed over to the Viceroy of Egypt. The inhabitants depend for their water supply on two or three wells about a mile from the town, and also on rain-water, which is collected during the wet season in a large sort of reservoir at the same place. The supply is at all times limited, and the quality of the water not particularly good, being strongly impregnated with salts. Towards the close of the dry season, when the water becomes very scarce, it turns thick, and is dark brown in colour. During the early autumn the climate is almost deadly for Europeans, and the natives themselves suffer greatly from sickness, the most prevalent complaints among them being dysentery and enteric

fever. The shallow lagoons and damp marshy
ground all round the north-west side of the
town add considerably to the unhealthiness of
Suakin. When the tide, which is only slight in
the Red Sea, runs out, these lagoons are left exposed to the burning rays of the sun, and as they
are full of filth and refuse of all sorts, the overpowering stench that arises from the foul black
mud, festering and fermenting in the heat, simply
defies description. The most unhealthy time
of year is from August to the end of October,
and during this period the battalion of Marines
quartered here since May last had not unfrequently twenty per cent. of their strength sick ;
and at one time the percentage rose as high as
twenty-five. In September, the ratio of sick per
month, that is, men who passed through hospital,
was equal to fifty per cent. of the total strength.
During the ten months, counting from May
last year to February this year, fourteen hundred
men passed through this battalion ; that is, a
total of fourteen hundred men either died or were
invalided during a short period of ten months.
The weekly returns from which I have collected
these statistics were prepared for the information of the officer commanding the battalion,
who was in Suakin the whole time himself, and

who kindly allowed me to look through them.
The facts, therefore, are unimpeachable, and
show a degree of suffering concerning which
people at home knew nothing at the time, and
know little now. The returns referred to were
most carefully made out, and amongst other information contained in them, I noticed a calcu-
lation of the per centage of sickness as applied
to the age of the men. The cases were divided
into three heads—men under 25 years of age,
men between 25 and 35 years, and men between
35 and 45. I found that at least sixty-five per
cent. of the total number of cases occurred among
the men under 25 years of age, while the men
between 35 and 45 escaped with comparative
immunity. Of the fourteen hundred men who
passed through the battalion, by far the greater
number were lost during the unhealthy season,
that is between August and the end of October,
and I found that from the 15th of November
to the 27th of February, there were only 333
fresh admissions into hospital, the strength of
the battalion during this period averaging about
520 of all ranks. The battalion was split up
into various detachments, and the amount of
sickness was materially influenced by the position of the detachment. In this way those

who suffered least were those quartered at the
Right Water Fort, some two miles out from the
town ; while the detachments at Fort Ansari
and Island Redoubt, nearer the town, suffered
most. The prevalent diseases were enteric
fever, intermittent fever, simple continued fever
(including typhoid), dysentery, diarrhœa, and
debility, under which head were included affections from the sun.

Such, then, is the effect of the climate of
Suakin on Europeans, and the above figures
are a fitting monument to what the British
soldier is called upon to suffer for Queen and
Country. I have no wish to be an alarmist, and
long ere these pages appear in print, I pray
that the English soldier may have left these
shores, never to return. I mention nothing
about the actual number of deaths, because,
although a great number occurred at Suakin, by
far the greater number took place at sea,
between Suakin and Suez. There was often a
difficulty in sending the worst cases away in
time, as the vessels available were few, and in
this way many valuable lives were lost that
might have been saved. There were, of course,
many who recovered when they reached home,
and numbers of these were not permanently

lost to the service, but the after effects of
climate are too well known to need a reference
here. We had a sad experience after the
Ashanti War, for I remember men being invalided and discharged two years after we had
returned home, entirely owing to the germs of
disease gathered on the Gold Coast.

But let us turn from this somewhat depressing
subject, and go back to Suakin itself and its
surroundings. There is one thing I omitted in
dealing with the climate of Suakin, and that is
the rainy season. They generally count upon
rain during November or December, but the
heaviest rain does not last more than about two
days, when it comes down in real earnest and
true tropical fashion, and in a way quite foreign
to all but those who have experienced it. This
one great downpour is followed by showers,
which occur now and then, but by no means
frequently. The climate is not unhealthy during
this season, as it is in so many places during the
rains. The temperature is highest during the
month of August, and the highest point reached
by the thermometer last year was 125° Fahr. in
the shade ; this was on the 20th of August. The
official record of the temperature kept by the
Royal Engineers on Quarantine Island gives

the *mean* temperature during August last as
follows : maximum 116·10°, and minimum 90·70°.
On looking through these returns I found that
in this month there were six days when the temperature was over 120° and thirteen on which it
was over 116°, while there were only two on
which the maximum temperature was below 100°,
and on both these the thermometer stood at 99°.
After the middle of September the temperature
became slightly lower, but there did not appear
to be very much difference between the two
months. I shall refer to the temperature that
we experienced during the campaign further on.

The population of Suakin is very "mixed."
There are Arabs belonging to all the neighbour-
ing tribes—Hadendowas, Amaras, Fadlabs, Beni
Amers, Bisharems, and Shaharibs. There are
also a number of Soumalis.

They are quite black in colour, and naked
with the exception of a white cloth worn
round the loins. The women, at least some of
them, cover their faces with a thin white
material, which they wear wound round them
and over their heads. These are mostly the
married women. They all wear gold ornaments
in their noses and ears. Certainly the opera-
tors who made the holes in their noses to

support these ornaments had no qualms about
the destruction of beauty, for if they had
bored them with an augur they could not
have been more roughly done. Some of the
women I saw, and who were not troubled with
any superfluous clothing, had their hair done in
curious fashion ; the commonest way, though,
appeared to be to wear it in a great number of
very thin, straight twists, about as thick as an
ordinary pencil. These twists were about six
inches in length, and each one preserved in a
thick plastering of grease. The men's heads
were much more curious, though ; I noticed some
who wore the hair frizzed till it stood out fully
six or eight inches on either side of their
heads. This extraordinary thick growth, half
hair half wool, was then parted over each ear
and round to the back of the head, the hair
below the parting being brushed downwards and
outwards, and that above the parting upwards. A
long wooden pin or thin stick was run through the
top part of this erection, and the effect was complete. The Arab boys had their heads shaved
with the exception of one tuft of hair, which was
allowed to grow long, and this tuft was generally
on the side and towards the back of the head,
and gave them a very rakish appearance. Many

of these little chaps are really nice-looking, with
cheery faces and bright sparkling eyes. Their
cheeks are almost always ornamented with three
long slashes on each side, done with some sharp
instrument when they are very young. I saw
one or two little girls of twelve or fourteen years
of age who were far prettier than I ever thought
it was possible for blacks to be. They lose
these good looks, though, almost entirely as
they grow older.

The population of the place varies a good
deal; but, counting Italians, Greeks, and Egyptian
soldiery, there must be at the time I am writing
little short of eight thousand people here.

One of the chief points of interest to us in
Suakin was Osman Digna's house; not that
there was anything particular about the house,
either inside or out. It stood close to the
water's edge up a small creek on the south side
of the town. A stick cut from Osman Digna's
garden was considered a great trophy.

Most people now know Osman Digna's history,
but for those who do not it may be as well to
give a short sketch of his antecedents. This
person, then, was born at Rouen, and is the
son of French parents, his family name being
Vinet. He was called after his father, George,

and began his education at Rouen, but after a
while was moved to Paris. A few years after
this his parents went over to Alexandria in connection with some matter of business, and shortly
afterwards his father died there. His mother
then married a merchant of Alexandria, Osman
Digna by name. This man took a great fancy
to his step-son, young George Vinet, and brought
him up as a Mohammedan, sending him to complete his education to the military school at
Cairo, where he had for his companion Arabi.
Here he studied tactics and the operations of
war under French officers. It was at this period
that his father-in-law migrated to Suakin, where
he set up as a general merchant and slave-dealer,
and very shortly was doing a very lucrative
business. At his father-in-law's death George
Vinet continued to carry on the business under
the same name. A few years passed, and when
the war broke out in Egypt, in 1882, Osman
Digna espoused the cause of his old friend and
companion, Arabi, and became one of England's
bitterest foes as the Mahdi's lieutenant. In
appearance Osman Digna is a fine-looking man,
tall and well-proportioned, though rather fat.
He wears a long black beard, and has lost his
left arm. He never gets on a horse, and in the

D

few engagements in which he has thought fit
to risk his valuable life he has always been
present on foot. As for the Mahdi, the prime
cause of all the misery and bloodshed of the
past four years, he is, I believe, the son of a
carpenter, and a native of Dongola. His proper
name is Mohammed Ahmed, and he was born
about thirty-seven years ago, and is much the
same age as his lieutenant. In 1870 he went to
live at the island of Abba, where he gained a
great reputation for sanctity, and gradually collected a great number of holy men or dervishes
around him. His subsequent actions are now a
part of the history of the last five years of bloodshed, and call for no recapitulation here. How
long he may be able to retain his position as the
true prophet is a matter of doubt, but it is to be
hoped that the poor deluded Arabs may be shown
the folly of being carried away by the professions
of a man whose sole aim is self-advancement, and
who is ready to sacrifice everything, his religion
included, for the attainment of this one end.

The Mohammedan religion appears to present
peculiar attractions to the native tribes in Central
Africa, and the false prophet is indebted for the
number of his recruits to the enthusiasm of the
converts to Mohammedanism, with whom the

idea of the regeneration of Islam by force of
arms is amazingly popular. The teachings of
the Mahdi may be summed up as follows : universal law, religion, and equality ; destruction of
all who refuse to believe in his mission, whether
they be Christians, Mohammedans, or pagans.
The causes of the rebellion have been ascribed
to the unjustness and venality of the Egyptian
officials, the suppression of the slave-trade, and
the military weakness of Egypt.

It was noon before we were safely piloted
through the treacherous inner reefs, some of
which run out only two or three feet below
the surface. The channel had been buoyed out
by the sailors, and an officer came off to bring
our ship in. We eventually made fast to shore
half-way up the channel leading to the inner
harbour, and right abreast of the English cemetery, which consists of a straight line of about
thirty or forty graves, each with a cross at the
head, some made of rough pieces of wood, and
some of iron. Almost all are ornamented with a
border of rough stones round them. This burial-
ground is only about thirty yards from the water's
edge, and is not at present enclosed in any way.
Since we have been here there have been men
at work perpetually digging graves at the rate

of two or three a day, so that there might
always be several ready. Whenever it has been
practicable we have always brought in our dead
and buried them here ; the officers being for
the most part buried in coffins, the men in their
blankets. There are one or two of the common
mimosa bushes among the graves, otherwise
there is no vegetation of any sort, and nothing
but the dry, hot sand of the desert.

We were all hoping we should be disembarked
that afternoon ; but orders were sent off to say
that this was to be postponed till the following
morning at daybreak. Some of us, therefore,
determined to try and get a boat and go
ashore, but it was with difficulty we did so, as
boats are scarce at Suakin. It does not seem
to have occurred to the native mind that a large
fortune might be made plying this trade. I
should be very sorry, however, to trust myself in
one of their very narrow canoes, which are of the
type one used to read of as a boy in Fenimore
Cooper's novels—mere long logs of wood hol-
lowed out and sharpened bow and stern. The
dexterity with which they handle these frail
craft is marvellous, and they go along at a great
rate, with the water very often within an inch of
coming over the side.

Our first object on landing was to find the post-office, and such a post-office it turned out to be—four walls and a flat roof, the floor of sand, the furniture a very rickety table, apparently made out of old biscuit-boxes. On this table and on the floor lay a pile of letters and newspapers a foot and a half high. We routed among these for some time without much result, so contented ourselves by handing to an Egyptian boy, who appeared to be in sole charge as the local postmaster-general, the letters we had brought ashore to post, feeling that they had a very poor chance of ever getting to their destination. On our way back to the wharf we passed a row of about fifty Arabs, all sitting in the same position, with their backs against a white wall. This being my first introduction to black and withal naked people, the contrast of their black skins against the white wall struck me as very funny as they sat in a long row in solemn and perfect silence, staring at us as we passed.

It is a curious thing how many ways there seem to be of spelling the name of this place. One sees " Suakin," " Suakim," " Souakin," " Sawakin," and many others ; but I believe, if one wished to be absolutely correct, the proper way

is "Savagin," with the "g" pronounced hard, as
in the word "begin." The Arabs have a legend
about the place, and the story they tell you is
as follows:—"Many hundred years ago a prince
came from the north bent on some warlike
enterprise, and, according to the custom of that
day, he carried with him his women. Among
them were seven virgins, who, before he commenced his further advance, he placed for safety
on the island on which the town of Suakin now
stands. Many months after the prince returned
to find his seven virgins the mothers of seven
children. No explanation being forthcoming he
christened the place 'Savagin' (*sava*, with, and
gin, a fiend or devil), literally, 'the place of the
devil.'"

I can only assure my reader that we found
the literal translation of "Savagin" to agree
perfectly in our minds with the opinion we very
shortly formed of the place.

CHAPTER III.

LANDING.

THE dawn was just breaking on Sunday, the 8th of March, as the barges came alongside to put us ashore. It was a most lovely morning, and the air so clear and bright that one could distinguish every feature in the mountains miles away inland. The sun was just showing itself above the horizon as we landed at one of the piers of Quarantine Island, and even at this early hour gave promise of the heat of the coming day. My company was sent on with a guide to show us where our camping ground was to be. We marched along the field railway for about a mile, leaving the town of Suakin behind us ; and as we advanced H.M.S. *Dolphin* opened fire over our heads at some groups of the enemy five miles away on the desert. We could see the great shells pitch and throw the sand up into the air thirty or forty feet high.

The mounted infantry were also out skirmishing ; and the first intimation we had that real
work had begun was passing a man lying in
a dhoolie, and wounded in both arms.

Turning to the left off the field railway, we
marched along parallel with the earthworks of
the town and about a mile from them, till at
length we were halted on a bare piece of sandy
desert—just a sample of the country for miles
and miles, except that there was no scrub—and
told that we were to start marking out our camp,
and that tents would shortly be sent out to us.
We accordingly piled arms and let the men take
off their kits, as it was uncommonly hot.

We had provided each of our men with a
piece of bread and a quarter of a pound of
cheese ; so this, with a suck from a water-bottle,
made an excellent breakfast. We had to wait
a long while before our tents made their appearance, and it was ten o'clock before the first string
of camels arrived with a part of them. We
were all soon at work, though, and in a couple
of hours we had transformed our bare patch of
sand into a smart camp, all alive with the hum
of many voices and the bustle of men getting
everything ship-shape.

Our tents were certainly excellent, and were

those known in India as "European privates'."
These tents are made of a thick white cotton
fabric, and are double, so that, I think, no sun
could ever get through them. The roof of the
tent is supported by two stout bamboo poles
standing about six feet apart, and there is a
space of a foot or more between the two thicknesses composing it, both of which are again
lined, the outer one with a deep maroon-coloured
material, and the inner one with a pale yellow.
A wooden bar connects the two poles, and forms
a useful place for hanging things upon. The
walls of the tent are about four feet high, and
are made in four pieces. There are thus four
doorways to the tent, each having an awning
over it, which is fastened to the roof and supported by two bamboo sticks. This awning
can be let down and the walls closed in at night
if desired. As we had expected to find ourselves
under double bell tents of the home pattern, we
were agreeably surprised. We were four officers
in a tent, so had plenty of room, the inside
measuring about eighteen feet by twenty-three.
The men were about twenty in a tent.

We arranged our tent in this way—a camp
bed in each corner, with our kit-bags and spare
baggage along the walls. We drew an ordinary

deal barrack table out of store and put this on
one side of the pole bar; on the other side was
our mess-box, the top of which served for a side-
board.   Our swords, belts, and water-bottles
we hung on pole straps, and the floor we
carpeted with the sacks in which the tent was
packed on the march.   We had each brought
a camp-stool, so these completed our furniture
and added materially to our comfort.

About noon some mules arrived, bringing our
rations of bouilli beef and biscuit—also some ten-
gallon tins of water.   This was all very quickly
served out and swallowed too.   The bouilli beef
is the ordinary tinned stuff, and always went by
the name of "iron rations," to distinguish it from
fresh-meat rations, which we got sometimes twice
a week.   The biscuit is very nasty, and quite
uneatable unless stewed in some way, as it is as
hard as steel.   We always used to stew our beef
and biscuit up together, putting in any fresh
vegetables we could get—such as potatoes and
onions, and occasionally some pumpkin.   This
concoction we called "soup;" and precious
nasty soup it was too, even when swamped
in Worcester sauce, or eaten with chutney or
pickles, of which we had brought a plentiful
supply.   On days when we had no fresh vege-

tables served out, we had at first each a ration of lime-juice, which was excellent stuff, to my thinking.

In the afternoon I went into the town and had a look round, and much to my delight found one or two houses where all manner of tinned provisions were sold. These were kept by enterprising Englishmen, and a wonderful business they must have done with us soldiers. The best one was Ross's, but there were others which fell little short of this. It was here I discovered some really good white bread, which I promptly bought and carried back to camp in triumph. There was, however, not much use in buying this afterwards, as the ration bread served out to us was very good, though rather bitter, and we always had plenty of it.

By the time I got back to camp our horses had all come in, and were being picketed in rear of our tents. Some of them looked a bit tucked up after their voyage; but this was not to be wondered at, as they had had a roughish time of it. They all pulled round but two, both these having been very bad at sea.

I ought not to omit to mention that during the interval two men arrived in camp, of foreign and uncertain origin, bringing with them something which always appeals at once to the soldier's heart—a barrel, of beer ! Having obtained leave to sell to the men, the amount being limited to a pint a man, they very soon came to the end of their barrel, no doubt with a handsome profit to themselves. The cask bore the homely and familiar name of " Bass," but the liquid that issued from the tap would have astonished any member of that excellent firm ; it was dark in colour, as thick as pea-soup, and as sweet as treacle—which last, indeed, it rather resembled. But Thomas Atkins is not to be denied ; beer is beer to him, and he is not over particular about the taste, more especially when the cask is labelled " Bass," and he is four thousand miles away from home and in the middle of the desert.

Having watered our horses and posted our guard and sentries, we had another turn at the " soup," and then lay down for the night in happy ignorance of any danger. We heard a few shots about eleven o'clock in the direction of the 70th camp, and in the morning were told they had had two men wounded and one killed. This was the first of those memorable night attacks which were afterwards the cause of so much misery to us. I don't think any of us got much sleep after our hard day's work, for the heat was tremendous, and I lay all night with the perspiration pouring off me. The first part of the nights were generally very hot, as the wind which blew in from the sea during the day dropped altogether. Towards morning it became quite cold, and one was glad to get under a blanket.

The next morning we were up before light, and out and about getting everything into its place. We generally had a cup of hot coffee or cocoa at half-past five or six o'clock, and then breakfast about eight, when there was more soup for those that liked it ; but I am thankful to say we had brought plenty of sardines and potted meats with us, so there was an alternative.

At this time the force was composed as follows : The 70th (East Surrey), who were encamped about half a mile to our left front and close to the Right Water Fort ; their camp, like ours, being completely isolated from the rest of the force. To our right front and about a mile away lay the 49th (Berkshire), and behind them were the Royal Marines and a battery of Horse Artillery. Further in rear still was the Head-quarter camp, and between us and them lay the Medical Staff camp at " H Redoubt."

The Indian Brigade was on the south side of

the town ; our camp was all on the north-west
side.

The Medical Staff were at this time under
single bell tents, and suffered severely from the
sun. I never saw fellows more sunburnt in so
short a time, for they had only arrived the previous day ; and some of them came over to us,
complaining bitterly about it, as well they might.
One of the newspaper reporters mentioned this
in his telegram home, but the press censor
struck it out as not the case. Seeing is be-
lieving, however, and there were the single bell
tents right enough. Even at home in summer-
time a bell tent is almost unbearable, but under
a tropical sun it must have been frightful, and
never ought to have been allowed for a moment.
They had a few double bell tents, but the sun
came through these just as severely as through
the single ones.

Our camping-ground was by no means well
chosen ; it was down in a hollow to begin with,
and therefore damp. The sand, so close to the
sea as we were, and on so low a level, is full of
salt, and in the mornings the floor of the tent
was always quite wet. The first night we hung
our clothes up in the tent, and the next morning
they were all wet through from the moisture

rising from the ground. Only one of us was foolish enough to put his clothes on in this state, and suffered by getting a sharp touch of fever. After this we always, when we did undress—which was not often—put our clothes under our air pillows, and thus kept them dry. Another unpleasant fact connected with our camp was, that it was quite close to the Arab burial-ground, and there were some hundreds of graves within sixty yards of our tents. As the Arabs do not bury their dead very far beneath the surface, but rather on the top of the ground, with a covering of stones over the bodies, the atmosphere at nights was unpleasantly loaded with the foulest odours. This, one would have thought, was hardly a healthy spot in a hot climate for even a temporary camp.

Of course, we all very soon had the skin burnt off our faces, not only by the direct heat of the sun, but by the refraction from the sand, which is almost as bad. One thing which nearly all of us suffered from was sore lips. Our lower lips would swell up to an enormous size and then break and fester. It was very painful, but when once cured we were not troubled again in this way. A good thick moustache was the best preventative, and I am sure a beard protected one's face a great deal. Some few of us shaved, but nearly all let their hair grow. With all due deference to the remarks in "our only General's" (?) pocket-book, that it takes as long to clean a beard as to shave one off, I am inclined to think that a beard is by far the best thing on service. If cut once a week and kept short it is no trouble at all to keep clean. Another thing most of us did was to have our hair cut off quite short to the head, but I am not sure that this was a good thing. It was cooler and more easily kept clean, certainly; but in a hot climate a good crop of hair is a protection from the sun, hair being a non-conductor of heat.

Two battalions of the Guards arrived to-day (9th), and marched out to their camping-ground on the side of the field railway just beyond the 49th camp and in the direction of the West Redoubt. The camp of the Guards Brigade was at this time at right angles to the general run of the rest of the camp and in advance of it.

The next day there were more arrivals, and, in fact, all this week there was a constant stream of great transports coming into harbour full of either troops or stores. Gradually the whole of this side of Suakin was turned into one great town of white canvas, and unoccupied ground in

the morning was ere night transformed into a
scene of busy life. Long strings of camels were
to be seen traversing the desert in all directions,
bringing up supplies of all sorts to the camp
from Quarantine Island. Fatigue parties were
marching here and there, or toiling under the
burning sun. Mounted orderlies galloped over
the plain, and generals and staff officers visited the
different detached camps and inspected the fresh
arrivals. Down at Quarantine Island there was
indeed a busy scene. There men of all nation-
alities worked night and day like great swarms
of bees, unloading the transports as they arrived
in quick succession one after the other—at one
time full of stores and equipment, at another
of forage and fuel ; at a third, perhaps full of
camels from Berbera or India, when each camel
had to be slung up from the hold and swung
over the side.

At last Quarantine Island contained something of all sorts—tons of railway plant, camel-
saddles in thousands, harness, gigantic cases
full of clothing and equipment, mountains of
compressed hay, camels, mules, horses, tents,
ammunition, and a thousand other things, a list
of which would fill a volume. We had to work
and toil, to be sure, from daybreak to sun-

E

set, in the sweltering heat of that foul harbour,
the air filled with dust and the sickening odours
from the fœtid swamps around, with the shouts
of the niggers as they slaved in a state of
nudity, and with the roar of steam and the
scrunch and rattle of a hundred donkey-engines!

Those were days not easily to be forgotten;
there were stirring times coming, and we all
worked cheerily and merrily enough as we
looked forward to the day of the general advance, and the chance of a good fight with
Osman Digna and his hardy followers.

The most disagreeable part of the work at
Quarantine Island was unloading the camels.
These long-suffering creatures are by no means
sweet at any time, more especially after having
been crowded up in the hold of a ship, where
red mange has spread among them, and where
fleas and ticks have multiplied innumerably.
Our camels were from all parts. The finest
to look at were those from India. They were
much taller than either the Egyptian or the
Berbera camels, some of them being nine feet
to the top of the hump, and were able to carry
heavier loads; but for all this they were nothing
like so handy as the Berbera camels with their
Aden drivers. We could form these up in

lines of twenty and march them abreast, but
the Indian camels were generally marched four
in a string, one behind the other, and thus it
was difficult to close them up so as to occupy
as little ground as possible. The camel is a
curious sort of beast, and he gives one the impression of being in a chronic condition of low
spirits. He grunts and moans in a doleful way
when made to lie down or stand up, and at
night gives vent to the most awful sounds, something between the roar of a bull and the grunt
of a boar. As to his capabilities as a beast of
burden, he is, no doubt, admirably suited to the
ordinary requirements of desert travelling ; but
many of us thought we should have done better
had we had more mules. The Indian brigade
did the greater part of their own transport work
with mules during the campaign, and of course
we had many hundreds too, chiefly from Cyprus,
and driven by natives from that island. Our
ammunition column was composed almost
entirely of mules. An average camel carries
a load of four hundred pounds, and though
an Indian camel can carry more than this, it
is unadvisable ever to attempt to overload him.
We found three hundred pounds quite enough
for the little Berbera animals, and also for the

Egyptian, some of which last were too small and
too young to be of any use, and never ought
to have been bought even at a push. Loading
a camel is not so easy a thing as it sounds, and
though it depends mainly on balance, it depends
also greatly upon the position of the load, and
the lashing of the load in the *celita* to the saddle ;
unless great care is taken, a sore back will ensue,
and the camel be rendered useless for some
considerable length of time.

Many people labour under the idea that a
camel can and will, with comparative comfort
to himself, go for a considerable length of time
without water. That he can do so I do not
wish for one moment to deny, but that he does
so only with a corresponding loss of power was
apparent to us all at Suakin.

General Gordon has stated that in his experience camels have lived without water for
as long a period as nine days ; there is, however,
no doubt that when in hard work and hot
weather camels should, whenever it is possible,
be watered twice a day. Seven to eight gallons
a day is a fair allowance for them, but this may
be greatly increased with advantage.

Many of our camels were driven with the
ordinary nose-rope and nose-peg, but I think

this unnecessarily cruel, and though it is a
check on refractory animals, I see no reason
why an ordinary running nose-band should
not be amply sufficient. Some of our camels
were vicious, but not many of them ; a few were
kickers. The bite of a camel is very severe, and
their kick, even with their soft feet, is quite
sufficient to break a man's leg. When you see
a camel open his mouth and give vent to a loud
gurgling sound, a large red-coloured inflated bag
as big as a good-sized melon appearing at the
same time from his throat, my advice would be,
to those who are strangers to camels, to stand
off! A well-bred camel may be known by the
fineness of his coat and the smallness of his
hind feet.

The camels from India came accompanied
by native drivers, and a certain number of transport officers from the Indian Transport Staff.
These drivers 'were a mixed lot, and for the
most part understood their business well. They
worked well enough under officers who could
speak to them in good round Hindustani,
but one would have to be a linguist indeed to
speak to each different class of drivers in his
own language. There were among them natives
from all parts of India—Punjabees, Sidiboys,

Bengalees, Scindees, Pathans, Hindoos, and sundry others.

The Aden drivers, Soumalis, with the camels from Berbera, were hardy fellows, and of course well used to the climate, caring as little for the sun as the Arabs themselves. You would see them going along with their camels during the hottest hours of the day with no covering to their shaven heads, and no garments except the white cloth round their waists.

It was curious to count up the number of different languages one heard spoken in and about Suakin at this time. Besides English, French, Portuguese, and Italian, there were amongst others the following : Turkish, Arabic, Somali, Greek, Armenian, Hindustani, Punjabi, Gujarati, Bengali, Mahrathi, and Pukhtu.

There was another native Indian corps—the Bhisti corps, water-carriers, composed mostly of Punjabee Mussulmans and Punjabee Hindoos. These were capital fellows to work, and did good service.

We often used to talk, as we looked round on all these vast preparations and this great concourse of men of all sorts and conditions, on the enormous outlay of money that was being spent without stint, on the toil and sickness and death

around us, and we used to wonder then what it
was all for. We knew that, being soldiers, we
went where we were told, and did what we were
told when we got there, but beyond this I do
not believe there was a man in the whole of this
magnificent force who could have given you any
intelligible reason for which we were fighting, if
indeed his ingenuity enabled him to give you
any reason at all.

And yet there we were, a picked force, armed
with every scientific means to effect our end—
everything, from an air balloon, with its gas compressed and brought all the way from Chatham,
to mule batteries of screw-guns, Gardners, and
rockets, and to rifles of the most perfect pattern
and greatest rapidity of fire. And all this to
war against what? A foe worthy of our steel?
Yes, undoubtedly yes. Armed? Yes; but with
spears of the rudest make, with swords of the
days of the Crusaders, with shields of crocodile
skin, and with a certain number of Remington
rifles which they scarce knew how to use. A
foe fighting with all the wild pluck and determination of their race, and supported by a
fanaticism which turned them into men who
courted death for two reasons—first, because it
transferred them to a happier land; and secondly,

because they preferred it a thousand times to a
life which might show them their freedom gone,
their land wrested from them, and their race
decimated.

CHAPTER IV.

NIGHT ATTACKS.

WE received orders on the 11th of March that we
were to shift our camp, and I was sent off to the
Camel Depôt to get a hundred camels and fifty
Aden drivers.

The Camel Depôt was inside the town lines,
and was always the scene of much activity, as
all camels, horses, and mules were taken there
on being landed, and then turned over to the
various departments and brigades on requisition
or order, when they were numbered and branded.
A more pestilential place it would be difficult to
imagine, for all round it there was an expanse
of open cesspools and stinking swamps. The
native town was quite close round it, and the
collection of filth from the huts was simply
indescribable. There were some thousands of
camels there that morning, and a perpetual
stream of fresh arrivals was continually pouring

in. There were camels of all sizes and shapes—
camels from India, camels from Berbera, from
Upper Egypt, from the Sûdan, and from any
other part of the world where camels were to
be bought and sold. Some were strong-looking
animals, and others weak and thin, while some
had already given it up as a bad job and succumbed to the hardships and privations. Their
drivers, too, of every hue and nationality, each
wearing a tin medal bearing his number, were
hustling these wretched animals about, whack-
ing them with sticks, and getting them up to
the picketing-lines. Their screams and holloas
added to the general state of noise and confusion. Interpreters roared the orders in a variety
of languages, and officers at their wits' end
endeavoured by superhuman efforts to establish
something approaching to order. Add to all
this a scorching burning sun, deep sand, clouds
of dust, and every one running down with sweat
and begrimed with dirt, and you may have a
faint idea of what sort of place the depôt was.

I had a terrible job to thread my way through
the line of camels to the commandant's tent, as
the mare I was riding was simply terrified at the
sight of a camel, and resorted to every trick she
could think of to get rid of me and get out of

the depôt; added to which she was quite
unbroken. So, to say the least of it, it was hot
work.

It took a long time before my hundred camels
were picked out, and then I formed them up in
line against a wall, and made them lie down
while I went round and inspected them with the
Soumali headman, who was to accompany me.
It was with feelings the reverse of pleasant that
I at length gave the order for them to follow me,
as I could not help wondering, first, how I was
to get the long string of animals through the
maze and confusion in front of me, and second,
how I was to retain possession of my mare
(which by this time was nearly mad with fright)
and keep my eye on the camels at the same
time.

Like many other things, we achieved it at last,
and as soon as I got outside the town I halted
to allow time for stragglers to come up.

The drivers now had a difference of opinion
as to whether they were being led in the right
direction, and, unfortunately, I laboured under
two difficulties with them that day, as I could
not speak a word of their language, and, moreover, was entirely unarmed. I had been on
foot up to this, my horse being led by a couple

of friendlies, who, I could see in the distance,
had their work cut out for them; but I now
again determined to mount, and see what could
be done towards pushing along, as we had two
miles to go to the Ordnance Store camp, to
draw saddles and equipment for each animal,
before they would be of any use in transporting
our camp and baggage to our new ground.

It was midday before I got back to our camp,
where I found all the tents struck. We were
soon hard at work loading up, which we found
very disagreeable work and somewhat difficult,
as we were quite inexperienced. Sometimes we
had to load a camel three or four times over.
First, one would get up before the load was
adjusted; or perhaps, with another, the load was
too heavy for him, and he would not rise at all.
Then, with a third, a part of the saddle would
give way, frighten the camel, and off he would
go at a gallop, gradually kicking himself free,
and smashing up saddle and load as he went.
Then two men would have to go and catch him
and bring him back, when a fresh saddle would
be fitted, and a load beautifully balanced would
be put upon him. Then he would get up when
his head was let go, and, with an awkward lurch,
round would go the load under his stomach.

Tommy Atkins would sit down on the sand then, and scratch his head and look at the animal in front of him with despairing eyes, as much as to say, " I wonder what your next little game will be."

By half-past six we had pitched our camp again on a fresh site, and on the extreme left flank of the front line. The position of the various regiments was at this time somewhat peculiar. There appeared to be no particular system about it, and we were told that military requirements had been allowed to sink before sanitary considerations in choosing the camping-grounds.

It appeared to us as if every one had been allowed to take his choice, and regimental camps were scattered about pretty much like plums in a cake, and with just about as much foresight on the part of the chief cook.

The front line, two miles from Suakin town, was taken up by a chain of redoubts running from the Right and Left Water Forts on the left to the West Redoubt on the right. Both of these were signal-stations, and rendered quite impregnable by deep ditches and Gardner guns. The redoubts were circular-formed, and surrounded by a ditch ten or twelve feet broad, across which ran a plank which could be drawn

inside at will. The line of the camps started
from the Right Water Fort, where we were,
and extended to a point about two miles away
and half a mile in rear of the West Redoubt.

Two regiments of the 2nd Brigade, the 70th
and 53rd, were on the left; then came an interval
of a mile or more to the Guards Brigade, which
ran at right angles to the front; the Coldstream,
Grenadiers, and Scots Guards camps, being in
line facing towards the Water Forts.

In rear of the Guards came the Sandbag
Battery and the camp of the 49th. To their
left rear was a battalion of Marines and a battery
of Royal Horse Artillery. Further to the left
was a part of the cavalry, the 19th Hussars, who
left us shortly after this. Then half a mile to
the right rear came the Head-quarter camp ; and
further back still " H Redoubt," the camp of the
Army Hospital Corps.

The Ordnance camp was a mile to the right
rear and close to the water's edge, while the 5th
Lancers and 20th Hussars were stationed in
rear of the centre of the line and about three
quarters of a mile from the town lines.

The Indian brigade, both cavalry and infantry,
were all encamped on the south-east side of the
town, where there was also a long chain of

redoubts and forts, the most important point being Fort Foulah, where there were some wells.

Thus it will be seen that the camps were much scattered, and placed in such positions that not only were they unable to protect themselves, but were a source of danger to each other as well, for, with the exception of the front line, there was no direction in which the scattered units could fire without endangering comrades in one direction or the other.

The Arabs were quite alive to our condition, and, with their consummate craftiness, took advantage of the folly of our dispositions.

It seems almost incredible that a trained force, and some of the finest troops in the world, should have been liable night after night to be "rushed" by a few savages. Nothing goes further towards demoralizing troops than a sense of insecurity at night. Men are unable to get proper rest, and without sleep, especially in such an enervating climate as that of the Sûdan, a soldier cannot be depended on in daytime either to march or fight in the way he should. Added to this, a perpetual series of night attacks, carried on by a few determined and reckless individuals under cover of the darkness, tended so to shake the

nerves of our men that the efficiency of the force
was to a certain extent undermined.

I must mention that there was a line of
pickets across the whole of the front, and these
were stationed in the redoubts. The interval
between these posts was, however, much too
great, and in the intense darkness that prevailed
at this time small parties of the enemy crept
along on the ground and passed through the
line without being detected by the sentries.
They were then able to traverse the intervening
space between the outposts and the camps, and
choose their points of attack.

The unoccupied ground already referred to
between the Guards camp and the two regiments
of the 2nd Brigade gave them free ingress, and
thus they were able to attack us in rear or on
the flanks at will.

On the night of the 7th of March the 70th had
had their rear-guard attacked, and had lost two
men wounded. After this we had no peace at all
at night, as directly it became dark the enemy
would open fire on us from a distance which
was not at all pleasant, or creep into our tents or
up to our sentries and stab a man or two before
we were aware of any danger.

The night of the 11th was one of the most

disagreeable of all, as parties of the enemy attacked ever so many points at the same time.

We had just sat down to our soup at about seven o'clock, when heavy firing was opened by our pickets, in reply to the " crack," " crack," of the Remingtons which was going on in front.

As the night wore on, every now and then a single shot would break the stillness, and then would follow a volley or two, when all would be again quiet. The dismal cry of the sentries, "All's well!" would be taken up by one post after another, till it died away in the far distance. This shouting of the sentries was very trying, as it alone rendered sleep impossible. The men would call out at their very loudest, laying considerable stress on the " all's," and cutting short the " well." They seemed to call out far more than was absolutely necessary, and for the sake of company more than for anything else. There was one great disadvantage besides in this calling, and that was that it enabled the Arabs to determine the exact position of each post. It was a relief to find that common sense came to our rescue for once, and the next morning an order was issued putting a stop to the practice, and also doubling each post, so that, by being two together, the men had more con-

F

fidence, as one was able to patrol to the next post on the right or left, while the other kept a sharp look out.

About midnight the firing grew heavier, and as we stood in front of our tents we could see the Sikhs in our rear hard at work, while firing was going on up at the Guards camp and also right away in rear at the Ordnance camp.

By 2 a.m. the whole of the front line of pickets were blazing away as fast as they could, and then there rose a cry that the pickets were coming in. Immediately bugles and trumpets sounded the "fall in" and the "double," and then there was the rush of many feet and the dull sound of many voices as men ran to the posts told off to them in case of attack.

The firing ceased for a time, and the pickets fell back on the main body, not without some loss. A patrol of two men and a corporal were set upon as they were retiring, and only one man escaped, the others being killed. They were marching back with their arms at the slope, when some of these daring fellows came up behind them, pulled them over backwards by their rifles, and immediately despatched them, only one of them, with a frightful wound in his face, escaping with his life.

No sooner had the pickets come in than a terrific fire was opened all along the line, and the many detached camps in our rear appeared to be having a merry time of it too, for their bullets came most uncomfortably near us.

To add to the weird appearance of the night, the *Dolphin* threw the electric light far and wide across the country, making everything which came under its rays as bright as day. At one time a whole camp would suddenly be shown up distinctly, perhaps a mile or more off, and one could distinguish the men standing to their arms or firing away only too probably at some imaginary foe. Then in an instant our camp would be illuminated as if by sunlight, and every feature of the ground would be as distinct in our front as at twelve o'clock in the day.

This light, to our thinking, had its disadvantages as well as its advantages, and I am not at all sure that, under the existing circumstances, the former did not kick the beam. In the first place, the path of light thrown was not more than about thirty yards broad at a distance of two miles, and if by chance it happened to be directed on a party of the enemy, they were very soon put out of sight again as the light swept across the ground. They could also, by

lying down when they saw the light approaching, completely evade observation, as they had
a trick of covering themselves with sand in a
moment and leaving nothing visible but their
heads. Sometimes the light was moved suddenly from point to point, and when this was
done parties of the enemy were occasionally
shown up and advantage taken of it immediately.
The sailors working the light on board the
Dolphin were, of course, unable to see when they
hit off a point suspected by us on shore, and
often and often after we had been peering through
the darkness at what we took to be moving objects,.
the light would cross us, and, before we had
become accustomed to its brilliancy, would pass
on and leave the darkness doubly dark.

The gravest fault connected with the light
was that, from its position, it enabled the enemy
to take note of our movements, as it showed up
the various camps from time to time. I not
unfrequently saw the light turned on to a suspected point of attack, and kept there for five
minutes or more, when, of course, everything
coming under its rays, the whole way from the
ship was thrown up into light. In this way
one could see solitary sentries or small pickets.
standing at their posts like so many statues.

I have no wish to derogate from the enormous advantages to be derived from this most useful scientific appliance, for I believe it to be invaluable. But I do wish to point out that its utility is proportionate to the position from which the light is thrown. Placed as we were, there was no alternative but to use the light from one of the ships in harbour. The *Dolphin* was lying right away to our rear, and two miles from our front line, so that the enemy, I am inclined to think, reaped more advantage from its use than we did, except in certain instances.

For the light to be used with the greatest effect it should be thrown from a point on either flank, thus sweeping the whole of the front of a position, and, so to speak, enfilading it. It should never be in rear of those for whose advantage it is being used, if it can possibly be avoided, as in throwing the light to the front it is bound to show up everything from the point where it is being worked. By working it from a flank the additional advantage is gained that the whole of the ground in front of a position is illuminated at once, instead of a space of thirty or forty yards, as it is then broadside on.

Modern science has not revealed to us at

present a perfect mode by which we can be absolutely independent of steam power in generating an electric current of any strength ; but when a thoroughly complete system of storing electricity has been invented, there is no doubt that apparatus for electric lighting will form a part of the equipment of every army, just as much as it does now every ship of war.

We stood to our arms for an hour or more, but the Arabs appeared to have drawn off, and contented themselves with firing a few shots at us at long range, resulting, so far as we were concerned, in one casualty only. Soon after this the day began to break, the firing ceased, and we were soon beginning another day of ceaseless toil.

Our killed were buried in front of the redoubts, where we found many traces of blood, but no dead. The Arabs always carried away their dead with them, so we were never able to arrive at what execution we had done. The firing had been very heavy off and on all night, and there is no doubt they must have had many casualties.

I was told afterwards that the Sikhs did some execution, and that a party of Arabs returned five times to try and fetch away one of their number who had fallen dead close to the tents.

The detachment in charge of the Camel Depôt had also a rough time of it ; they were up all night under a heavy fire, but, being behind the town lines, escaped without any casualties.

The most determined attack that night was made on the Ordnance Store camp, where there was some severe fighting.

This camp, as I have already said, was in rear of all the others, close to the water's edge, and adjoining two landing-stages or piers. Deep water close up to these piers enabled ships of considerable draft to come alongside and unload in the same way as at Quarantine Island, and all stores in the way of equipment and ammunition were landed here—clothing, arms, boots, helmets, blankets, harness of all sorts, pack-saddles, camel-saddles, carts of all sorts, sizes, and description ; tents, storage-tanks for water, portable tanks and barrels, miles of telegraph wire, cases of stationery by the hundred, ammunition for all arms ; and, in fact, anything and everything that could possibly be wanted by an army in the field.

It may be imagined, therefore, that many hundred thousand pounds' worth of stores were collected at this depôt, and it appeared that the enemy were fully alive to the importance of the place. In the creek behind the camp lay the *Dolphin* and the *Carysfort*, but the camp itself was almost entirely unprotected by any form of earthworks or laager.

I had occasion to go down to the Ordnance camp the next day, and received the following account of the fight from the senior Ordnance Store officer in command there, which I think it better to put as nearly as possible in his own words. His story of the fight ran as follows :—

"When I first arrived at the Ordnance camp on the 8th of March, it consisted of four Indian double-poled tents and a sepoys' tent. Enormous quantities of camp equipment and stores of all sorts were pouring in in an endless stream from early dawn to late at night.

"The depôt was scarcely safe from attack, and very weakly defended by a laager of Maltese carts on the north and west sides only, the east and south sides being left open.

"It had been protected up till then by a nominal guard of one non-commissioned officer and twelve men at night-time, but I had this increased to one non-commissioned officer and twenty-four men of the 49th Berkshire Regiment, which at this time were finding the guard. It

was generally believed that the enemy would
never venture to penetrate so far in rear of our
lines, especially as we were under the guns
of the *Dolphin* and *Carysfort;* still, I never
could see why they should not make a circuitous march, round by the sea-shore, as there
was a wide stretch of open ground a mile and a
half in extent between the right of our lines and
the coast.

" My tent was pitched between two others on
the north-west side of the depôt, the men's tents
being on the east side.

" I slept alone in my tent, and felt in perfect
safety until the night of the 11th of March, when,
to our astonishment, we were suddenly attacked
by the Arabs under Abdul Adab.

"I usually let my candle burn out on the
table, and kept all four doors of my tent open,
but on this particular night, luckily for me, my
candle blew out. I had slept soundly all the
first part of the night, and until I was suddenly
aroused by rapid firing and most frightful yells.
I realized at once that we were attacked, and
looking out of the door of my tent, saw distinctly
some black forms moving about the yard on
all-fours.

" A few seconds afterwards, hearing somebody

rushing towards my tent, and not being able to find my sword in the darkness, I ran out of another doorway and scrambled under the curtains into the next tent, where I narrowly escaped being shot by one of my own brother officers, who luckily though recognized my voice as he was going to fire.

"As we came out of the tent a sentry ran towards us, calling out that we were surrounded. I then managed to get back to my tent, and found my revolver and sword, when I immediately joined the guard, who I opened out into skirmishing order. We then marched, or rather felt our way in the darkness, through the cases and bales of stores from end to end of the yard, every now and then coming across a wounded man as we went.

"The electric light was then suddenly turned on us by the *Dolphin*—it had not been going before this—and the scene which presented itself to our eyes was one of awful horror. Two sentries had rushed in mortally wounded; one had dropped down dead, while the other was standing up, simply hacked to pieces, and bathed in his own blood, but without any sign of consciousness.

"It was with a sense of relief that we heard

the ships lowering their boats, and soon after they came alongside, and landed a party of blue-jackets and a doctor, who conveyed the wounded back on board.

"By this time the enemy had made off, leaving their leader Abdul Adab dead on the ground. He had made across the yard to my tent, and was shot in the back by one of my men; but this only partially stopped him, for he hurried on and was eventually bayoneted by a man of the guard, who was himself cut down at the same moment.

"His death evidently stopped the whole force outside coming down upon us.

"There was a considerable force seen when the electric light was turned on, hurrying away to the north-west, but the guns of the ships were unable to open on them for fear of the camp.

"Their idea was evidently to surround us, as, while one party attacked the guard in front, another party came round between us and the water, and entered the yard from that side. Their reserves were held in readiness to complete our destruction as soon as the first attack proved successful.

"I am afraid the guard in the first instance

was taken by surprise; the outlying sentries were pounced down upon before they could give the alarm, and most of the men of the guard were wounded as they came out of the guard-tent.

"Had it not been for the determined bravery of the men, who one and all behaved splendidly, our losses must have been very great; as it was, we had three men killed and eight wounded.

"Abdul Adab was a very fine-looking man, at least six feet two inches in height, and magnificently proportioned; he wore the ordinary white blouse, but had many ribbons across his chest, which we took to be decorations. He was afterwards recognized as Osman Digna's standard-bearer."

A report was current after this that Osman Digna had sent in word to say that if we would return the body of Abdul Adab, and not burn it, he on his part would undertake to forego all night attacks in future; but I am not able to vouch for the truth of the story. The body was not returned, but buried about a hundred yards in front of the Ordnance camp.

As to the losses sustained by the Arabs on this occasion, many traces were found of bodies being dragged away along the ground, and

when the mounted infantry went out the following morning on their line of retreat, they came
across many of their dead which had been
dropped when the electric light had been turned
on to them.

On the principle of shutting the stable-door
after the horse had been stolen, means were
at once taken to strengthen and defend the
Ordnance camp. Earthworks were thrown up
all round it, and strong parties of Egyptian
troops were at work digging deep ditches and
throwing up high parapets. These ditches soon
filled with water, owing to the low level of the
ground, and in a few days the stench there was
frightful, and moreover was the cause of much
sickness afterwards among the Ordnance Store
Corps.

We were very hard at work all the next day
getting our horses up from the Camel Depôt.
Most of them were English horses, and therefore
unsuited to the climate, and they were, generally
speaking, a seedy-looking lot. Many of them
were unbroken, which fact did not lend to the
pleasure of riding them in a hot climate. It
would have been far better if we had had
nothing but Arab horses for riding purposes,
and mules for draft-work. Most of the horses

we brought from England succumbed to the climate before very long. The mounted infantry were mounted on Arab horses, and had much the best of it over the rough ground. A part of our cavalry afterwards took over the horses from the Egyptian cavalry regiment at Suakin, who were also mounted on Arabs.

Night came again, and with the darkness the ball reopened and the bullets began to whistle over our heads. It was evident that we were to have no peace.

There was a large outlying picket of the 70th posted about four hundred yards to our front, and this kept firing away all night.

About one o'clock in the morning we suddenly heard a tremendous row going on just in our rear, and we thought at first that a party of the enemy had entered our horse-lines, but running out of the tent we found that the rear-guard of the 53rd were being attacked. It was always very difficult to make out from whence sounds came at night; the air was so clear that you could hear people shouting as if they were close to you, when in reality they were a mile or more off.

This attack on the rear-guard of the 53rd was a most audacious proceeding on the part of the enemy. The guard, fortunately for them, were lying down outside the guard-tent, while the double sentry patrolled up and down about fifteen yards in front, and behind a low-shelter trench. All at once a party of some fifteen or twenty Arabs, who had crawled towards them in the darkness, jumped up, rushed up to the parapet, fired a volley or two into the guard, and then disappeared again immediately. The guard, who were under arms in a moment, fired in the direction of their retreat, but, so far as could be gathered, without effect. The casualties among the guard were three men wounded, while a fourth had his rifle knocked out of his hand by a bullet which passed straight through the stock.

The night wore on, and our time was taken up going round our sentries and looking about, expecting every minute to be attacked; and again we got no sleep.

Firing was going on in every direction; and the bullets continued to hum and to whirr through the air, while many came through our tents.

We would not allow our men to fire, though they might have done so with perfect safety. We had begun during the day to throw up a

shelter trench across the front of our camp, and
we lined this with some of our men that night.
It was three o'clock when we saw about a
hundred yards to our front what we took to
be something moving, and many of the men
wanted to fire, but the order given in a low
whisper was—

"Steady, men ; wait till you can see the white
of their eyes."

We were all lying on the ground, almost
breathless with excitement, when we could see
that, what some had thought to be bushes, were
indeed a party of the enemy crawling stealthily
towards us.

"Present," in a low tone, then a pause to
allow for a steady aim, and then, "Fire ! "

There was a cry and a shriek in front as the
volley was thrown in, and then there was silence
again. We gave them another, though, where
we took them to be, and the next morning there
was little doubt that some at least of our bullets
had found their billets. So far as our camp was
concerned we were not troubled again that
night, but we had no sleep.

I had to go down to Quarantine Island at
daybreak to superintend the disembarkation of
a shipload of camels from India, and was at

work all day long at the job. I managed to secure a good breakfast though on board the vessel, the first I had had for some time.

The camels were packed pretty tight both on the upper and lower decks, and the smell of them was simply sickening. They were slung up from below by steam, and then dropped on an inclined plane and driven ashore. A native driver accompanied each three camels, and before the middle of the afternoon we had them all on the wharf and picketed inside the walls of the town for the night.

It was just growing dark as I got back to camp after a very hard day in the sun, and I would have given a good deal for a wash, but water was scarce, so I had to go without.

We began to take the firing at night now as a matter of course; and so when the bullets began to fly about again we took little or no notice of it, only passing a remark or two such as " They are beginning a little earlier to-night," or " No rest again, —— it ! " It was uncomfortable, though, letting alone the want of sleep. Lying all night long, either waiting for an expected attack, or peering into the darkness till every bush in front took the form of a man on the move, began to tell on our nerves. Then there

G

was that sense of insecurity and the uncertainty
of what might happen in the night, for none of
us knew when we lay down at night whether
we should be alive in the morning.

I was lying on my camp-bed with my sword
on and my revolver ready to my hand. It must
have been about half-past ten o'clock, and I may
have been dozing. There had been no firing
for an hour ; and now that the sentries had been
stopped calling " All's well ! " the quiet of the
camp was only broken by the neighing of a
horse or the grunt or moan of a camel, when
suddenly the stillness was interrupted by the most
awful scream that it has ever been my lot to
hear—a loud, long wail of agony, as of a man
mortally wounded, crying out with his last
breath. It was a sound that absolutely seemed
to curdle the very blood in one's veins. Then
came a rush through the camp as those men
who had been in their tents turned out. A few
random shots were fired without effect, and the
enemy, if ever seen at all, had disappeared.

With the stealth of a wild beast, and with the
wriggle of an eel, a party of Arabs must have
entered the camp unnoticed by the sentries, and
then rushing in through one door of a tent have
stabbed and hacked with their long spears as

they rushed through and out of the tent the other side. One poor fellow had been stuck with a spear right through the stomach, and with a last frightful and pitiful yell had expired at once.

How the Arabs managed to enter the camps we never discovered ; but this sort of thing was repeated by them over and over again in the face of double sentries and guards and pickets all over the place.

We had a most uncomfortable night of it after this. Some of the enemy had got round . in our rear, between the Water Forts and the cavalry camp, and had been sighted by a party of Indian infantry on the one side and the cavalry pickets on the other.

I had noticed, as I was coming home that night, that three circular redoubts had been thrown up on three sides of the cavalry camp, for what purpose has always been a complete mystery to me. What use they could possibly be nobody ever knew, as the cavalry camp was in rear of the centre of the front line of the encampment, and men firing from these redoubts at all must, in spite of every precaution, have fired into some camp or other either in front or to the right or left.

However, on the night in question, they were manned by the cavalry pickets. Whether any of the enemy really did get round in our rear I am unable to say ; but there is no doubt that the men at this time fired at everything, and when they were not sure whether they saw anything or not they gave it the benefit of the doubt, and let fly.

In this way we very nearly suffered severely, and how we escaped being all killed is a mystery. Suffice it to say that we stood up there and watched the Indians fire volleys by squads clean into us, and we could count the number of men firing by the flashes, as they were not more than five hundred yards off. The firing from this side must have been infectious, for we very soon afterwards found ourselves under a cross-fire from the cavalry redoubts on the other. A pleasant variety of bullets were now cutting up the ground at our feet—the Indians, firing with Sniders, and the cavalry with Martini-Henry carbines. Our chief work was to prevent a stampede among our horses, but I am thankful to say the firing at length stopped before any serious damage was done, and we came out of action with our friends with the loss of a mule only. We, on our part, put the whole thing down to General Funk's account, as we saw nothing ourselves, and never fired a shot.

The main cause of danger was of course the utterly unsystematic arrangement of the camp, which could not have been too severely condemned, and it was generally considered that we ran more risks on account of our friends than we did on account of our enemies.

Our General arrived the next morning, so we all began to look forward to an advance being made very soon.

The whole force was now complete, and all the troops had arrived. Only one thing was not ready, and that was the water transport. We had plenty of transport animals, but nothing to carry water in ; no tanks, or barrels, had as yet arrived from home, and it was impossible to move the force without the first requisite for an army operating in such a climate.

It was a most magnificent sight certainly, looking round the country from our camp in the early morning, for the Right Water Fort was the highest point between Suakin and the hills. Miles of tents were spread over the desert in every direction, like so many scattered hamlets. Long lines of camels and baggage animals traversed the plain, bringing up stores and

munitions of all sorts, and mules were to be seen
drawing water-carts up to the front with the
supply of the precious fluid for the day.   In
the distance the white houses and squat towers
of Suakin, with the harbour crowded with any
number of gigantic transports, which seemed
almost to dwarf the houses with their enormous
proportions. Behind the town one could see
the low flat shores and surf-washed coral reefs
of the Red Sea, trending away miles and miles
to the southward till they were lost in the hot
brazen mists of the horizon.   On the other side,
that is towards our front, there was nothing but
the flat, hot, inhospitable desert, with its ragged
patches of wild growth, and its clumps of mimosa
thorn bushes scattered here and there, far and
wide. Only one thing relieved the monotony
of the scene in this direction—the mirage, which
at this time of day was always most striking, as
it converted parts of the desert into a series of
beautiful lakes, with objects of fantastic form
reflected on their smooth surfaces. A line of
bush would be turned into a strong line of
entrenchments, while a clump of mimosa often
took the form of some outlying fort, or work of
great strength. Behind all came the magnificent
range of mountains brilliant in a deep crimson

colour, and standing up against the hot sky with a dark purple outline. There was a marvellous clearness in the atmosphere in the early morning, and every detail of the mountains could be seen as far off as forty miles or more. It was at this time of day, too, that the sailors stationed in the tops of the men-of-war in harbour very often sighted parties of the enemy retiring towards Hasheen after tormenting us all night. When they did it was not long before a "boom" was heard, and a great nine-inch shell went hurtling through the air, aimed with unerring precision at a range of nearly six miles. A dull echo of the shot and a column of dust thirty or forty feet high told us of their position, but we could never see whether the shots took effect or not, though there could not be much doubt about it.

We were hard at work all day branding camels, each animal having to be marked with the Broad Arrow and a distinguishing number. It was a tedious and tiresome job, but the camels bore it with their accustomed resignation, and we only had one accident during the several days we were at it—our farrier sergeant getting a kick from a vicious one full in the face. As fast as they were numbered they were sent off on various fatigues, bringing up rations or fire-

wood for the various regiments of the brigade.
Every bit of firewood we used out there was
brought hundreds of miles by sea, as there was
none to be had in that part of the Sûdan.

The days seemed very long, and owing to
the harassing night attacks both days and nights
appeared to be mixed up.   Want of sleep began
to tell a bit on the men, but we had very little
or no sickness, though we were toiling all day
long, and watching and being shot at all night.

A curious order came out at this time, but
I am unable to say how far it was ever carried
out.   Each man was to be provided with a
cartridge or two, the bullet of which had been
cut into four pieces, and these were to be used
at night "pending the arrival of buckshot
cartridges from England."   The idea was a
good one, but we thought it somewhat of a
slight on the men, as it was of course done to
get over the danger of one camp firing into
another.   The men ought never to have been
allowed to fire at all, or even to load their rifles.
The bayonet was quite good enough, and several
battalions out there gave up firing at night
times altogether.   We were firmly convinced
ourselves that a great deal of the firing was due
to shaky nerves, and many a bush got a hot

peppering because of its imaginary likeness to a " Fuzzie."

I went out one morning in front of the redoubts to look at a point at which there had been some heavy firing the night before. It was a raised mound of sand where, when first we came out, a picket was always stationed. On the top of this mound stood a barrel filled with sand, behind which the sentry of the picket was posted. This barrel stood up against the sky line at night and in the darkness might have been taken for anything, and certainly resembled a crouching figure, as one of the staves had been broken and stuck out from the side like an arm.

This old barrel must have had a very hot time of it, for it was simply riddled with bullets; I counted thirty-eight shot-holes, and when I emptied it, among others, I found a shrapnel bullet, so all arms must have had a go at the barrel, and it was certainly very satisfactory to see how many of the shots had been successful.

We had now been four nights without sleep, and should have been very grateful to the Arabs if they would have kindly given us a night's rest and agreed to carry on the war according to ordinary principles. But not a bit of it; no sooner had we finished our evening meal than the firing began again, and another night was spent lying in the trenches, and watching till daylight came again.

We only allowed half of our men to sleep in the tents, the other half sleeping behind the shelter trenches ready to repulse any attack in a moment. We had also at this time one or two "friendlies" of the Amarar tribe, who kept watch with our men during the night. The extraordinary keenness of eyesight possessed by these people we thought might have been of use to us, as they appeared to be able to see in the dark very nearly as well as they could in the daylight. Several times over they made signs to us that they could see figures moving across our front, and even became quite excited about it, and entreated us to shoot, but we could see nothing. It was very curious to watch them, but somehow I never felt any trust in them.

These "friendlies" wore a scarlet serge blouse and carried spears and shields, and they were regularly in our pay. I am not at all sure, though, that these fellows did not strip off their red shirts and carry to Osman Digna's people a complete account of our strength and proposed movements, and many of us thought that the so-called "friendlies" in Suakin, who were

suffered to walk about the place fully armed
and to come and go as they liked, were the very
fellows who made the night attacks on our
camp. No native should ever have been allowed
to carry arms unless he had been regularly
enrolled among the natives in our pay.

It was no uncommon sight just before sunset
to see groups of armed natives coming out of
Suakin. Where they were going I for one
never knew, but I should have been very sorry
to have met them after dark. In the face of the
acknowledged treachery of these people it was
curious that no attempt was ever made to put a
stop to this sort of thing ; but we English are a
confiding people.

CHAPTER V.

PREPARATION.

WE were getting tolerably accustomed to being
out in the sun all day by this time. The
weather was very hot and the sun shone down
upon us with never a cloud in the sky to
mitigate its rays. It set at night in a sky of
the deepest crimson, and rose in the morning
again to scorch us, to burn us, and almost sear
us with its horrible power.

I often used to think of the old country at
home, where the sunlight was a blessing, and
then look round on this bare, bleak, desolate
desert, where life was not, and where the sun
was a curse, where pestilence and fever were
hatched by it, and where men fled from it to
escape, if it were possible, its pitiless power.
And yet we toiled on beneath its rays ; we rose
in the morning and had done many an hour's
hard work before the sun showed above the

horizon of the Red Sea yonder. But we did not rise in order to get the work done before the heat of the day, but in order to crowd more working hours into the twenty-four.

It was wonderful to see how "Tommy" made himself at home. You would see him carrying on an energetic conversation with a native, and making up for his deficient knowledge of the language by talking at the top of his voice, and of course always addressing the native familiarly as "Johnnie." Then you would see him trying to make a pet of a camel, or riding one as if he had never ridden anything else. A hundred different duties fell to his lot, cooking, branding, fatigues innumerable, digging entrenchments in the very heat of the day, pitching tents, going on guard, watching all night under a heavy fire, and many other things besides. He got through them all, though, and was always to be heard chaffing and laughing, for he is a good fellow, Tommy Atkins, though he is bound to have a grumble and a growl sometimes, for "'tis his rights."

Among our most uncomfortable experiences were the sand storms, which came regularly almost every third day. The wind would rise and blow harder and harder with its hot breath

till the air became filled with fine sand. There
was no keeping it out of anything ; the whole of
the inside of a tent was covered with it almost
immediately and everything buried. Everything one tried to eat was full of it, one's eyes
and hair were full of it, it got into the water in
the covered tins, and worked its way through
one's clothes. If a tin of meat was opened it
was filled with the fine dust at once, and all our
food was full of grit and our bread spoiled.
Outside the tents the air was as thick as a
London fog, and marching in it nearly blinded
one ; but we had to work on just the same,
though it was very difficult to find our way from
one point to another. The goggles we had been
supplied with failed to keep it out, and the
veils were of little use, only sifting the dust one
swallowed a little finer, till eyes, nose, and throat
were clogged with it. The temperature during
these sand storms would generally be about 85° ;
so the dust used to stick to us and plaster
us, and there was little or no water to wash it
off. As a rule the wind dropped at about three
o'clock in the afternoon, and the air became
clear again.

It seemed to have struck somebody about
this period that a better disposition of the camp

could be made, and that probably the men might obtain a little rest at night if the camps were placed in such a position that they would be a support instead of a danger to one another.

Orders were accordingly given to close up, and we had a very busy time shifting all the camps into their new positions. The Guards were withdrawn and their camp pitched in the general alignment, their right-resting on Sand-Bag Battery. The 49th were shifted over to the right of the 53rd, and the Royal Marines next to them. This completed the front line, which thus ran from the Water Forts on the left to Sand-Bag Battery on the right. The head-quarters of the 2nd Brigade were shifted in rear of the 53rd, while the Head Quarter Staff were encamped between us and the Right Water Fort. The cavalry were moved up and en-camped about one hundred and fifty yards in rear of the 70th, and next to them on their right were the Mounted Infantry. Then came the Artillery and Engineers and a Field Hospital, " H Redoubt" being now turned into one of the shore hospitals. The whole of the Indian Brigade was withdrawn from the south-west side of the town and brought round and encamped in rear of our left, thus making a line of camps facing towards the south. This brigade was composed of the following regiments— 15th Sikhs, 17th Bengal Native Infantry, the 28th Bombay Native Infantry, the 9th Bengal Cavalry, and two companies of the Madras Sappers and Miners. Strength about 3000.

The strength of the whole force under General Graham must have been between ten and eleven thousand men, not including the native camel drivers.

The Indian regiments seemed to be much better off than we were, and the officers appeared to live in luxury; they went in for table cloths and glasses, and gave a very excellent dinner. The natives helped them out considerably, as they are by nature servants and cooks. They know how to make you comfortable under adverse circumstances, and certainly appear to be able to make a very good curry out of very little, though where the ingredients come from in the desert, I don't know; like French cooking, however, it doesn't do to ask too many questions. We gave a dinner party one night, and borrowed an Indian cook for the occasion. Our bill of fare we thought was grand :—Soup, pot au feu ; entrée, curry and rice ; pièce de résistance, more curry and more rice ; entremets, sardines ; sweets, preserved peaches. The whole washed down with a couple of bottles of dry Monopole. A cup of coffee all round followed, and a glass of whiskey before turning in, when we felt prepared for any number of Osman Dignas. Whether it was the above magnificent banquet, or that the Arabs let us alone, I only know that we went to bed, certainly, in our clothes, soon after ten o'clock, and never woke till a little before four o'clock the next morning. There was a faint idea, though, that the changing of the camp may have had a little to do with it. The enemy may have thought something was up, as they watched our movements of the previous day ; they certainly never fired a shot, and I suppose took a rest too, after their extraordinary feats of unexampled temerity.

The result was good all round, as we had our first sleep for five nights. There are limits to everybody's power of endurance, and the want of sleep after the exhaustion of the day was beginning to tell on some of us very much. With good food and plenty of water, men can stand hard work night and day ; but with indifferent food, and no variety from the daily ration of bouilli beef, there is bound to be a

H

certain loss of power in a climate like that of
the Sûdan, even with the strongest.

Before leaving home there had been great
talking about moving the army into the hills at
once, and thus getting the troops into a good
climate. Five minutes at Suakin would have
shown any one the utter impossibility of this.
People talk at home as if it was as easy to
move an army from one point to another as it
is to move chessmen ; and as simple to feed the
army when you get it there, as it is to feed a
party of school children, or to carry out the
arrangements for a picnic on the banks of the
Thames. The general tone of the conversation
was something as follows :—

' " Well, of course the climate of Suakin is hot,
but then you see as soon as you get there you
will be moved at once to Sinkat, and stop there
for the summer. The climate is a beautiful one,
very bracing and very refreshing ; in fact, you
will be quite well off."

Now, setting aside the enormous and gigantic
amount of labour entailed in moving even a small
body of say three thousand men over a short
distance of six miles, and maintaining them at
any particular point, when every ounce of food
and every drop of water has to be carried on

camels—it may be imagined at what cost it would be possible to move an army twelve thousand strong "at once," to a point thirty-six miles off, through a trying country, covered with a thorny bush and huge black boulders, rendering progress more and more difficult at every step, and with the chance of being hourly attacked by a determined foe constantly on the watch to take advantage of any laxity in your movements.

The convoy of camels to carry stores for even a day's supply is prodigious, and the rate of progression so tedious, owing to the difficulty of preventing any straggling, that not more than a mile and a half an hour can be traversed with any certainty.

As far as the climate of Sinkat goes, it is of course far preferable to that of Suakin, and comparatively healthy ; but the difference of temperature is one of degree only, as it is exceedingly hot in the summer months, though upwards of three thousand feet above the sea.

There was plenty of talk, too, about the ease with which a railway could be laid, and the wildest rumours were afloat about the rate at which the work would progress. Of course the army would be moved to Sinkat, and of course nothing would be easier than for supplies to be run out every day from Suakin.

The contractors or agents employed by the Government were not much behind the troops in their arrival at Suakin, and two or three days after we landed several transports entered the harbour with their cargo of five miles of railway plant complete in every detail ; and before we had been there a week, the British navvy was to be seen laying the sleepers and fixing the metals. The first part of the line was easy enough. The ground was firm and perfectly level, and so the work progressed with vigour ; but it was a different matter when the sandy, bush-grown country beyond the camp was reached, and "drifts" had to be cut through the thorny mimosa. All this—the severest part of the work—fell to the lot of the army. The line was ballasted by the soldiers, the sleepers were carried forward in carts by our transport animals, and the rails had to be dragged from the point up to which they were brought by the train, by teams of mules or horses. The contractor's work, and that performed by the navvies, was merely placing the sleepers at the proper intervals, and fixing the rails. For this the navvies received the princely remunera-

tion of twelve shillings a day, and time work, a
free ration, and a free kit ; while our soldiers
received only as many pennies extra working
pay as the navvies did shillings. By the con-
tract, too, the firm undertaking the work were
to receive bonuses in all of £40,000, in pro-
portion as the various sections of the line
were completed.

The additional labour thrown on the troops
of guarding the head of the line, and the work-
men during their labours, was also extremely
heavy. Nothing could possibly have been
worse for the men than this. They were exposed to the sun, and had nothing to do but
stand about and think. A few tent roofs were
sent out to protect them from the sun, but it
was not always possible to use these.

I do not think more than from a thousand to
twelve hundred yards were laid in a day over
this, the easiest part of the country, from Suakin
to Handub. The rate of progression in the hills
would necessarily be reduced, and at this rate
the line would probably reach Berber by the
end of August next year, or in other words, the
army would have been dragging its weary way
along a track, exposed to a thousand hardships
and privations, for a period of something like

seventeen months, the distance from Suakin
to Berber being not unfrequently traversed by
camels in ten days.

Another thing. It would be absolutely impossible to build this railway on the telescopic
principle—that is, making the railway carry all
its own plant forward as it goes—if, indeed, this
principle ever worked at all, and also to depending upon it for all the supplies of the army as
well.

Under these circumstances the impracticability
of running a railway over the thirty-six miles
from Suakin to Sinkat, if, indeed, we were ever
intended to move in that direction, may be
imagined.

There is no doubt that the combination of the
civil and military element in the attempt to lay
this railway was a mistake. Either the railway
should have been laid by the Engineers, as was
first intended, or else it should have been carried
out by a firm of contractors, representing a finan-
cial company in England, backed, if you wish it,
by the Government, and protected in their work
as far as possible by English troops.

A party of about eight hundred coolies had
been collected by the Royal Engineers in India,
for the purpose of laying this line. Most of

these men were experienced hands, and used to railway work. They were brought from India to Suakin, and proved of the greatest use, as they worked exceedingly well; but it was ridiculous to put this body of men, with their officers, under the orders of the contractors. Friction was bound to take place, and the experiment failed, and was therefore entirely given up.

The railway, to our thinking, was much too clumsy and heavy to be rapidly laid; and instead of a 4 feet 8½ inches gauge being adopted, the lightest possible form of railway compatible with stability and strength should be selected as the one for general use with an army, so that it would not only be very portable, but more applicable to rough countries, where sharp curves are often a necessity, and where gradients are of frequent occurrence.

During the Afghan war we were able to lay a light railway at the rate of a mile a day, but greater rapidity than this would have to be attained, and a mean of at least three miles a day would be none too much to expect.

The officer in charge of the line of communication found his hands tied in dealing with the contractors, as he was forbidden to interfere in any way with them; and though they on their

side were only too ready to accept the help of
the soldiers, without which they would have
been at a standstill, it was impossible that a
large civilian element could pull with the military, unless they were to a certain extent under
military discipline, and for that reason under
the same rules and regulations as the soldiers.
Thus, again, it was found impossible to get along,
and the work was accordingly retarded.

I am the last to discount the British navvy.
I admire his many good qualities, and above
all, his gigantic proportions and muscular deve-
lopment. I have always looked upon the navvy
as one of the grandest types of our race, and I
think if I were asked to bring forward a number
of representative English working men, I should
recruit among the navvies. But with all this, I
am bound to confess that the navvy as seen at
Suakin was not a success. Highly paid, well
looked after, easily worked in comparison to the
soldiers, and well fed, there was still a deal of
grumbling, and none, or very little, of that cheery
self-sacrifice and readiness to work of which we
saw so many instances among our own men.

I sincerely hope that the many failures in
connection with laying the Suakin-Berber Railway may be the cause of the authorities at home

taking seriously into consideration the advisability of organizing a regular Railway Corps.

A certain number of men attached to the Royal Engineers should be perpetually undergoing training in the various branches of railway making and railway-engineering. Opportunities at home are always close to hand, and could be easily taken up, and there should, therefore, never be any want of a field for operations of the sort. One thing is absolutely necessary, and that is, that the civilian element should in military railway laying be entirely eliminated.

Our wars are almost always carried on in countries not only without railways, but without roads. We have frequently been accustomed to make our own roads in war time, why should we not make our own railways?

With a force of trained officers and men as a nucleus, to be supplemented by paid native labour brought from India, or elsewhere, there should be no difficulty in carrying out work of this sort for an army in the field.

In these days of rapid movements, of quick concentrations, and short wars, every means offered by science, whether it be electricity, ballooning, or railway-making, should be at once adopted. We suffer ourselves to live in a

fool's Paradise indeed, if we put off all matters of
this sort to the day when we are actually called
upon to act. For the sake of " party," for the
sake of courting popularity, for fear of inter-
fering with monopolies and so-called " rights,"
and on account of a certain dread of what the
next election will bring forth, and how we shall
appear before our constituents with taxation on
the rise, we often forego spending money where
money is most needed ; and so, after having gone
in for a penny wise and pound foolish policy, we
find ourselves squandering our soldiers, shedding
our blood, and spending millions more than if we
had taken the stitch in time at first. " A standing army is a necessary evil " we are told ; if it
is so, do not be satisfied with spending a mere
sixteen millions and possessing a phantom, but
spend more and see that the money is well
spent. With our great colonies and dependen-
cies scattered all over the habitable globe, and
with all the many heavy responsibilities and
duties incumbent upon us by reason of our
vast possessions, the absolute perfection of our
army and our navy should always have our first
consideration, and a Ministry which, for fear
of risking popularity with the masses, allows
these two services to fall into a state of in-

efficiency, should be driven at once from office as unworthy of the confidence of the nation. A great writer has said regarding our country, that " while we have everything to fear from the success of the enemy, we have every means of preventing that success, so that it is next to impossible for victory not to crown our exertions. The extent of our resources, under God, is equal to the justice of our cause." A great war is looming in the far East, and the vibrations of a first shock have already sounded on our ears. Let us be prepared, therefore, while there is yet time.

> " I'll live to-morrow, 'tis not wise to say ;
> 'Twill be too late to-morrow : live to-day."

But I am digressing. We were all now looking forward to the general advance, which could not be much longer postponed. There was a sort of fever among the whole army to get on. Anything was better than lying in tents or trenches at night to be speared or shot at, and we one and all longed to be " up and at 'em." Our preparations were nearly completed, the water tanks and barrels had arrived, our stores were well up to the front, and yet there was delay, and we were condemned still to further days of waiting. Not that we sat with our hands in front of us, not a bit of it. There was always plenty of hard work to be done, and there always seemed to be too few hours in the day to get it all in.

I went up to the top of the Right Water Fort one afternoon to have a good look round the country with a fine telescope there was there, and very interesting it was. Half a mile to the front, and stretching right across to the West Redoubt, were our cavalry videttes and pickets. They must have had hot work of it, as they were out all day long standing nearly motionless in the sun. They had a few cases of sunstroke, which the doctors were pleased to diagnose as "exhaustion," and of course they suffered a good deal from sunburn.

There were one or two instances where men who had been out in this way all day, came in with a line across their faces as though cut with a knife, where the sun had caught them below the shade cast by the front of the helmet and opened the flesh.

Beyond the videttes were scattered groups of the enemy sitting or standing about, and perhaps waiting till darkness came on and they were able to make their customary descent on the camp. I could see them very plainly with

the glass as one of the party would advance
a little, evidently to take stock of what the
cavalry outposts were doing. Then after a
while he would return again, and there would
be a deal of talking and pointing, when the
whole lot would retire. They appeared to have
a regular system of outposts, and these parties,
consisting of from ten to twelve men, were to be
seen dotted about all along the front.

We had one of our first doses, about this
time, of the " Hgramseen," or " the wind of fifty
days." It is very unpleasant, very enervating
and very hot. This wind blows during this
season of the year, and lasts off and on for fifty
days, at any time of which it may be expected.
One very curious thing about the Hgramseen is,
that if it begins to blow one day it is absolutely
certain to blow for three days, but if it blows
over the third day it will continue till the fifth
day, when it as certainly drops again. I don't
know that it is an unhealthy wind, but it
seemed to take all the energy out of one, and
it was an effort to go about one's work. As a
general rule I was agreeably surprised with the
climate, and though the heat was intense I
could do a long day's work without feeling any
fatigue. We were feeding better now, and used

to send a camel down almost daily to bring up
tinned provisions from one or other of the stores
in Suakin. We got a variety of these provisions, and I think tried pretty well everything
ever prepared either by Messrs. Moir or Messrs.
Crosse and Blackwell. Our favourite things
were the Oxford sausages and the herrings à
la sardine, both of which were excellent. Stewed
beef steak, haricot mutton, mutton ragout, and
grouse *aux truffes*, were also among the most
appreciated. The tinned vegetables were not
at all bad, but we fought rather shy of these for
fear of colouring matter.

Never shall I forget one of our party returning one evening with two tins of *foie gras*.
Our delight was quite beyond description. We
sat down there and then, and with a good
allowance of ration bread very quickly put the
contents of the two tins out of sight. But there
is a sequel to this tale.

"Do you know," said our comrade, " I only
gave half a crown a tin for it ! "

" Dear me," rejoined we, " what a fool you
were not to buy more ! "

So it was settled that the very first thing the
next morning he was to ride back again to
Suakin and buy every tin he could lay his
hands on.

By eight o'clock he had returned from his errand, but with no *foie gras* for breakfast, much to our dismay, for I think we had all been repeating to ourselves, "*Foie gras* for breakfast, more *foie gras* for dinner, and still more for supper;" in fact, to our hungry insides it was to be "toujours *foie gras.*"

"Well," said one of us, who had been anxiously awaiting his return, "where's the *foie gras ?*"

"Well," answered our comrade, with a very long face, " I have been a bigger idiot than I ever thought I could be. Do you know that when I entered the store where I bought the stuff last night, the man rushed up to me saying, ' You are the officer who took the *foie gras ;* you are the officer who took the *foie gras.*' ' Yes,' said I, ' I certainly bought two tins of *foie gras* here last night and paid you half a crown for them.' ' Yes,' said the man in reply, by this time almost crying, ' I know you did—I know you did ; but they are half a sovereign each and not half a crown ! ' "

We retired to our tent then with heavy sighs, and contented ourselves with the dry bread which was to have had the *foie gras* on it. Perhaps it was just as well it hadn't.

One of our greatest failures with tinned provisions was with brawn.

"Who's for brawn this morning?" said our
mess president.

"Why, of course, we are all for brawn," we
replied.

The top of the tin was ripped off, and again
we were doomed to disappointment.

" By Jove, it's soup!"

And so it was, and yet it had been packed in
straw inside a large box. It was soup right
enough, though—nasty, thick, greasy-looking
soup, with pieces of white fat floating about in it.

Only one of the party tackled it, and he ate
his brawn with a spoon.

We heard one morning that a shipload of
oranges had arrived in harbour for the use of the
troops, and "when practicable," said the orders
on the subject, "an orange a day will be issued
to each officer and man." "This indulgence,
however," added the order, "is not to be looked
upon as a right." So for some days an orange
apiece was given to us, and very good ones they
were. I never knew what an orange really was
before, and no peach on a hot summer's day at
home ever tasted more delicious to us dried-up
mortals than did those oranges. We simply

devoured them, and felt inclined to eat peel and all.

I have never mentioned anything about our postal arrangements. We used to get our letters very regularly, considering all things, and though some necessarily never reached us, there was nothing to complain about. They only took ten days coming all the way from London, overland, *viâ* Brindisi, Alexandria, Cairo, and Suez, where a steamer of one sort or another met the mails and ran them down to Suakin. Every corps had its own letter-carrier, and a deal of sorting used to go on at the so-called post-office in Suakin, when the mail-bags arrived and were emptied out in piles on the floor. It was rather like looking for a needle in a truss of hay, and the letter-carriers did not, therefore, always wait till the whole lot was sorted out. In this way one sometimes got a letter two days afterwards, when least expected, and much to the delight of the recipient. When the detachment of the Post-Office Volunteers arrived, everything was very well managed, and much of the previous inconvenience as well as risk of losing letters, both going and coming, was avoided.

We always thought it very hard that we should be called upon to stamp our letters to avoid a

I

double rate of postage being levied on the
friends receiving the letters at home. I believe
this was claimed at first, though we used to
write in the corner, "On active service. No
stamps." Afterwards I heard that the ordinary
rate of postage was claimed on delivery of the
letters in England. It struck us as a little
severe that any charge should be made at all.
Surely letters from soldiers fighting hard for
their country might always be allowed to go free.
It is not much we get, and it would be a grace-
ful concession if this boon were granted in future.

Few people can understand the enormous
pleasure letters afford to soldiers on active
service. When there is so much work and so
many hardships to be undergone, a letter, giving
a glimpse of the old home, is an untold joy. To
hear about what they are all doing, what people
think about the war, or even the smallest details
of home life, all alike possess an interest quite
beyond comparison. The most trivial incidents
of everyday life are magnified in one's mind
into pieces of momentous intelligence, and
none of us, I am sure, ever found letters either
too numerous or too long. The lucky ones
who received letters sat down and simply
devoured them, and, with a happy smile upon

their faces, they would read and read till their
eyes seemed as if they would burn through the
paper, while they drank in the news of home,
of wife, of children. Reading the letters was
easy enough, but getting time to write them was
quite another thing. The only way was to have
a letter always going, and add to it as time
allowed.

Newspapers were a great blessing, and we
were quite as eager to see the news of the war
" on the paper " as the people at home were.
And here I feel bound to put in a word about
the " war correspondents." A more hard-work-
ing set of fellows I never saw. Up early and
late, they were always in the front where fighting
was going on, and always to be found where
bullets fell thickest and where danger was to be
met with. Then, after the fighting was over, or,
perhaps, after a long march, they would ride
miles in the hot sun and sit up half the night
to write home the doings of the day. There
always seemed to be a great spirit of rivalry
among the different representatives of the
press, and there was always a race among them
to get their messages off first. The people at
home ought to be very grateful to the war corre-
spondent, for he risks all, and sacrifices himself

entirely to supply news to be consumed daily at
the breakfast-table, or in the quiet and comfort
of some club armchair.   There is much that he
would telegraph home, if he could, but since the
appointment of a press censor, he is only able
to send exactly what that officer allows him,
and no more.   In this way many details which
should be known at home never reach there
until the reason for publishing them has passed
away.   What is forbidden in the telegrams is
naturally enough written in the weekly letters, but
by the time these get into print they are for the
most part stale news.   It is, of course, absolutely
necessary that certain restrictions should be put
upon correspondents for many reasons.   In these
days of universal cables, news of the movements
of an army is quickly enough sent home, and
there is nothing to prevent its being as quickly
sent out again for the information of the
enemy; but many unnecessary restrictions are
put upon correspondents which might be
removed, and many an item of news which
should be sent home is now stopped, because it
would, it is supposed, create needless alarm.   Oh
for the days of the immortal Russell !

Of all the thankless positions in an army
in the field, the press censor has the worst,

Abused by correspondents at the seat of war, maligned by editors at home, and continually found fault with by his superiors with the army for allowing too much to pass, he must have the temper of an angel, the tact of a consummate diplomatist, and the nerves and constitution of a Hercules, ever to carry on the work and live through it. For every single word that passes along the cables to the newspapers he is responsible, and every telegraphic message has to bear his signature before it can be sent off. Added to which he frequently has other duties of an arduous nature to perform, as those of press censor are combined more often with those of an officer acting on the staff in some capacity or another.

There were three figures which became very familiar to us in the camp. They were often to be met with together, and they would turn up at all times of the day ; in fact, they always seemed to be riding about somewhere, looking after some detail here or inspecting some fresh arrivals there.

The first of these was a very tall, broad-shouldered man, with a certain shrewd look in his face, with a kindly manner and a soldierly bearing. The double line of ribbons across his

jacket showed him to be a man who had seen
a deal of active service, and amongst his ribbons
was the most prized of all orders, though now
becoming a little too common. He always
seemed very grave, as if he bore on his shoulders
the weight of some overpowering responsibility,
and he certainly acted on the principle that
silence was golden, for he told his staff nothing,
and, they say, consulted nobody. One of his
personal staff once told me that they never
knew an hour beforehand when a move was
going to take place, and that this reserve was
carried so far that they never even knew what
time they were going to have their dinners.
Report put him down as a man who had studied
deeply, and who was well versed in the science
of war. His pluck in action and his excessive
coolness under fire were undeniable, but his
repute as a General was somewhat slender. We
all liked him because of his many attractive
qualities, and above all he was a true friend
and a perfect gentleman. He might have
been popular, but his somewhat cold manner
and habitual reserve rather repelled any
advances, and there was none of that spon-
taneous *bonhomie* and happy manner with his
troops, which, while it sacrifices nothing to dis-

cipline, wins for a commander the love of his soldiers.

The second figure was different altogether from the first. He was of middle stature, somewhat stout, and with a round, red, good-humoured face. He, too, wore many ribbons, and possessed also the red one of the Victoria Cross. He had a quick, sharp way of asking questions, and a somewhat "stand-off" manner with strangers, though when you knew him there was no pleasanter companion or kinder-hearted friend. He possessed also an attractive manner, and a cool, quiet way of taking things, which made him to a certain extent popular. He looked as though he had the constitution of a giant, and as if he could stand or go through with anything. He was always perfectly self-satisfied, and even when things went against him he acted as though it was all *couleur de rose* and rather a good thing for him. As to any qualifications to command—these were shown in after days. I ought to mention his right-hand man—a true soldier, an energetic staff officer, unhampered by rule and the trammels of red tape, and with the inestimable quality of perfect readiness to accept responsibility and total fearlessness of the consequences. Everybody liked him, and, though he had a quick temper, he never lost it, and if you wanted anything done, he did his best to help you, sinking personal considerations before all others.

As to the third, he was a short, sharp-featured individual, with a pompous and rather disagreeable manner, a loud voice, a quick temper, and a sense of his own importance which defied everything. He was not popular, and he seemed generally to be absorbed in that wonderful thought, "I am." A short answer was. all you ever received from him, and one which often fell far short of ordinary courtesy.

There was one thing which these three characters had in common, though utterly dissimilar in every other respect—one tie which bound them together as representatives of a fraternity—they were members of the same Society.

I mentioned just now the extraordinary way in which all projected movements of the force were kept a most religious secret, and how even the Heads of Departments never knew until sometimes half an hour beforehand of the intentions of our commanders. I cannot think that this was justifiable in the extent to which it was carried. Secrecy is an absolute necessity

very often in times of war, and especially so in a
country where the inhabitants are more than ever
quick to take advantage of any news they may
get hold of, and where a General is surrounded
by so-called "friendlies," always on the watch to
carry over to our enemies news of our intended
movements. I am perfectly ready to allow all
this, but I think that officers placed in a confidential position are entitled to consideration by
reason of that position, and, at the same time,
I think it is a slight upon the character of those
holding commands when they are not taken
into the confidence of their leaders. I do not
wish it to be inferred from this that I think
commanding officers and Heads of Departments should be at all times consulted,—far from
it ; I think that there would be a considerable
element of weakness in adopting for one moment
such a course. But I do think their convenience
should be at all times considered, for two reasons
—first, because hurrying may thus be avoided ;
and second, because their men may be saved
the strain of work attendant upon sudden movements. Let a General's movements be as
sudden and unexpected as possible—indeed, in a
warfare such as we were engaged in it is absolutely necessary that they should be so to ensure

success—but do not let this suddenness and rapidity of movement be attained at the price of a certain loss of efficiency, as well as much grumbling, when both can be so easily avoided. No department of the army felt the extreme inconvenience of this excessive reserve more than did the Commissariat and Transport. I often heard many of the senior officers of this branch of the service say that they knew nothing of what was going to happen, and that orders would come in to them one hour which had to be carried out the next. There is no doubt that in all branches of the service in the Sûdan much of the confusion, hurry, and annoyance caused by this mode of procedure would have been avoided if a certain amount of trust had been placed in commanding officers and Heads of Departments. If officers in responsible and important positions are not considered worthy of trust, it is high time that those holding such positions should be replaced by officers that are.

We all knew now that any hour we might hear the welcome news to advance, but we none of us had the least idea in which direction the advance would be, though we inferred it was not to be towards Sinkat, on account of the direction in which the railway was being laid.

That there would be fighting, and hard fighting too, we were well aware, and, from the cool way in which the enemy made his night attacks on us, it was evident that Osman Digna had not profited by the lesson we had given him last year—a lesson, too, from which we gained nothing, when we might as easily have marched on Khartoum and rescued Gordon as withdrawn to our ships. The opportunity then offered has never occurred again, and so through a mixture of vacillation, weakness, and total incompetence, we soldiers were for a second time sent forward to dye the desert sand red with our own and the Arabs' blood, and sow the burning plains thick alike with the graves of the Christian and the Mohammedan. Years hence the wail of misery which had its birth in all the bloodshed, the slaughter, the sickness, and the suffering endured by our soldiers in that blood-stained frying-pan, the Sûdan, will still find an echo in the land at home, where gaps in happy circles remain for ever unfilled, and where homes are blighted with the crushing weight of a sorrow that will never heal.

CHAPTER VI.

THE ADVANCE.

WE were going to advance; the day for which
we had all been waiting, working, longing,
for the past few weeks, was coming at last.
A renewed activity seemed to start up in the
camp, and men went about congratulating each
other, with a happy smile on their faces, that
they were not "going to stick here no more," as
they put it.

We knew nothing about what day it was
going to be, and of course all sorts of rumours
were going the round of the camp. At one
time it was going to be "to-night," the next that
it had been put off till "to-morrow at daybreak," and so on.

I was awoke on the morning of the 19th of
March, after a long night's work, by a friend
saying, "Come out and see the cavalry; they are
all out just in front of our camp." So up I

jumped, and, by way of getting a good view of
what was going on, ran up to the top of the
Water Fort, and there below me was as fine
a parade of troops as any one could wish to
see.

On the left was the whole cavalry force,
including the two squadrons of the 5th Lancers
and the 20th Hussars, the 9th Bengal Cavalry,
and the Mounted Infantry. Next to these were
the Indian Infantry Brigade, and on the right
were the three battalions of Guards, a battery
of Royal Horse Artillery being stationed with
the cavalry. After a short inspection by the
General, the English cavalry were thrown
forward, and gradually spread themselves out
over the plain like a great fan, the advance
parties keeping up a continuous flow of messages
to the main body by means of the ordinary
signalling flags. The 9th Bengal Cavalry acted
as a support and accompanied the guns. The
Indian infantry were kept out some time, in the
event of their being required, but the brigade
of Guards was sent back to camp. I do not
think I ever witnessed a more imposing spectacle
than was presented by the beautiful working of
this cavalry force, as they gradually felt their
way across the plain towards the mountains and

in the direction of Hasheen. The Mounted
Infantry were pushed to the front as the force
neared the hills, and a few shots were fired at
small parties of Arabs who showed themselves
from time to time.

It was considered probable that the enemy
would be found in force behind the isolated
hills which stand out on the plain in front of
the mountains, and behind one of which the
village of Hasheen is situated.

Our Mounted Infantry ascended cautiously
to the crest of this hill, on reaching which considerable bodies of the enemy were seen both
in the valley below and along the ridges in front.
Only a few shots were fired by the enemy, to
which our men replied. An Arab was seen to
fall here and there, as they retired up the
gorge leading towards the mountains, but they
never attempted to stand, and were evidently
only a part of Osman's forces, numbering in all
not more than a thousand men.

Hasheen was found entirely deserted. It consisted only of about forty wretched-looking huts,
a few of which had been evidently quitted in
rather a hurry, as there were remains in some
of a half-eaten meal.

A thorough examination of the ground was

made, and a well discovered. It was also ascertained that water could be obtained a few feet beneath the surface. The enemy never attempted to interfere with our movements, and by our sudden advance we had evidently taken him by surprise.

Before retiring, a letter from General Graham to Osman Digna was placed on a white stick in the centre of the village. In this letter General Graham referred to the respect that England entertained for all religions, and stated that it was her chief desire to maintain friendly relations with the Arab tribes, and to establish peace in the country. After referring to the defeats sustained by the Arabs at Teb and Tamanieb last year, the letter went on to advise the sheikhs to submit without delay, and thus escape the punishment and death almost certain to overtake them. This letter was in reply to one received by General Graham from Osman Digna a week or two ago, in which, after recapitulating his many victories and the defeats sustained by the Egyptians under Hicks and Baker, he advises us to withdraw before a like fate overtakes us and we are driven bodily into the sea.

Having thus completed our reconnoissance,

orders were given to retire. The village was
left as we found it, and, immediately our retire-
ment commenced, was reoccupied by the enemy,
who were seen all along the tops of the hills as
we marched back towards home. Our losses
were only one man killed, and one officer and
one man wounded. Two or three prisoners
were taken, and one of them, an old man with
white hair, was barbarously cut down by one
of the "friendlies" who accompanied the force,
before any one had time to interfere.

The whole force was back again in camp by
one o'clock in the day.

One word about the 9th Bengal Cavalry. A
more magnificent regiment no one could wish to
see. Their loose-fitting dress, made of kharkee,
with blue puttees instead of long boots, and with
blue-and-grey turbans as a head-dress, the appearance of these fine, swarthy-looking warriors
was enough to strike terror into any foe. They
were very grand-looking men and splendid
horsemen; but why were they ever sent to
Suakin to act as a Lancer regiment, when there
were so many splendid Lancer regiments to
choose from in India? Their arms are a sword
and a carbine, which they wear on a cross-belt
over either shoulder, but beyond a certain

amount of practice a few of them may have had in tent-pegging at regimental sports, not one of them had ever had a lance in his hand before. And yet they were sent off to Suakin to act as Lancers in the field, and use a weapon in action which is allowed to be one of the most difficult to handle, and which a man cannot be taught to use properly under two years of constant training and practice. What was the result? Having been provided with their staves through the philanthropy of a native prince when actually .on their march down country for embarkation, they arrived at Suakin knowing, naturally enough, nothing whatever about handling a lance ; and, to mend matters, two or three of the 5th Lancers were sent every day to give them instruction in the way to use their new weapon. Of all arms the lance is the best in warfare against a savage nation armed for the most part with spears, as it is a matter of necessity to keep the enemy at a distance. A sword is next to being absolutely useless against a spear and a shield, especially when these are in the hands of warriors who have been accustomed to handle them since their earliest boyhood. The result of suddenly arming a regiment in this way was that, knowing nothing about the use of the weapon, the men,

K

when in action, threw away their lances and drew their swords.

As regards the dress of the 9th Bengal Cavalry, they all wear steel-chain shoulder-bands, which serve as an excellent protection against a sword-cut. Some of our English cavalry officers had steel chains sewn into their shoulder-cords ; but why should not these be part of the regular dress of our cavalry, as it is that of the Indian cavalry ?

Just as the reconnoitring party were coming into camp, I was telegraphed for to go down, with another officer, to No. 5 Pier, where all the condensed water was pumped from the ships into large iron tanks on the wharf. I had no time to put any food into my haversack, as we had to be off at once. Moreover, the rations had not come up, so I could only take with me a box of meat lozenges. We were down at the pier, which was about two miles from our camp, in under a quarter of an hour, and there we found we had to collect on the wharf adjoining the pier several hundred tins, barrels, and mus-socks or water-skins, which were being landed at the Ordnance camp about a quarter of a mile off. We had to help us, a fatigue party of a hundred men from an Egyptian regiment, with four Egyptian officers and about fifty coolies. A well-known figure out there also accompanied us, and many were the nights of hard work we did together afterwards. A cheery voice, a happy, pleasant manner, a splendid constitution, and a man who never spared himself, he was more than popular with all of us. A civilian —he had never been a soldier—wearing a grey jacket decorated with the Cape medal ribbon, a round white cap with a peak in front and a curtain behind, and generally to be seen riding a small camel, his figure was familiar to all of us ; and some thought he looked a regular guy as he went about here and there, helping things along.

Our orders were to have thirteen thousand gallons of water loaded and ready to march by daybreak the next morning. With such material to work with it looked almost a hopeless undertaking, but it had to be done, and therefore must be done. A more miserable, indolent, useless lot of fellows than those Egyptian soldiers I never came across. Big men, most of them, but so lazy and so slack that it was utterly impossible to get them to move out of the slowest of walks, and their officers seemed unable to do anything with them. However, by dint

of a deal of driving and pushing, we managed
to get the tins and barrels on to the wharf just
as it was getting dark, and we also rigged up
six hand-pumps to pump the water out of the
storage tanks into the portable tanks. These
portable tanks were made of galvanized iron,
and were about three feet long, eighteen inches
deep, and eight inches wide. Each one held
twelve gallons and a half, and we put their
weight down, when filled, at 125 pounds. They
were fastened with a screw stopper, which could
be secured with a key. The barrels were of
two sizes—the largest held twelve gallons and
a half, and the smallest eight gallons. The
mussocks were water-skins bought in Egypt.
They were supposed to hold eight gallons each ;
but they leaked very much, and after the first
time of using them we always avoided filling
them if we possibly could. Who was responsible
for their purchase, I don't know, but they never
should have been bought. They were supposed to have been passed by a board of officers,
who sanctioned their purchase at one pound
apiece. Their value could not have been more
than a few shillings, and to us they were almost,
if not entirely, useless. The water, after it had
been in them a few hours, was absolutely un-

drinkable, and stank. The skins themselves
were covered with a brown grease, which stained
one's hands, and withal they crawled with vermin.

Just before sundown the camels to carry the
water arrived ; these were about seven hundred
in number, and we parked them in lines of fifty,
one behind the other, alongside the field railway,
a branch of which ran down to the pier.

A rather amusing thing occurred as the sun
sank behind the mountains. The coolies one
and all dropped on their knees, said their prayers,
and then made off at their best pace, as it was
contrary to their religion or inclination—I don't
know which—to work after sunset. We had no
time to run after them, however, so we let them
go. A fresh fatigue party arrived about seven
o'clock, and replaced the one we had been working with all the afternoon. As bad luck would
have it, this party was also of Egyptian soldiery,
scarcely less feeble than the first. No wonder
we administered such a wholesome thrashing to
them in 1882, and that they cut and ran directly
they saw the tops of our hats.

We began filling the tins at about eight
o'clock, and we managed it in this way. A pump
with indiarubber hose fitted to it was rigged up
in each of the large storage tanks into which a

constant flow of condensed water was pumped
from the condensing ships. Each of these
pumps was manned by two men, and two more
looked after the portable tins as they filled them
through an ordinary leather funnel, a third
screwing up the stopper and making it fast
with a key. Then a fresh supply of tins was
brought by another lot of men, who took away
the full ones and arranged them in rows ready
for packing into the trucks on the field railway.

It was not until late at night that we were
able to get an engine to draw the trucks up to
the place where the camels were parked. However, we did get one at last, and then we began
to run the tins and barrels up the line, and with
a part of our fatigue party to unload the train
again and place the tins in rows between the
camels, two in front of each animal, ready to be
put in the *celitas*, or nettings, later on.

It was very heavy work for us, as, though the
Egyptian officers did their best to make their
men work, we had to do the hardest part of it
ourselves, or it would never have been done at
all. If we turned our backs for a moment these
fellows would sit down on the ground, light
their cigarettes, and talk. It really was almost
maddening sometimes trying to get anything

out of them, added to which, only one of our
party could speak Arabic. We had begun the
night's work with one of the interpreters attached
to the army, but he became tired of the job as
soon as it got dark, and we saw nothing of him
again till morning.

It was now getting on for ten o'clock, and we
had been many hours at work without food, so
I suggested going across to the Ordnance camp
and begging a crust of bread.

I found my way over in the darkness, but my
friends there had nothing of any sort or kind to
give me, as they had eaten all their ration of
bread for their evening meal; so there was no
help for it but to return to the pier with empty
hands as well as empty inside.

I forgot to say that we were lighted in our
work by a lamp composed of five incandescent
lights hung from the top of a pole. These were
worked by "leads" laid on from the *Dolphin.*
They gave an excellent light, and I don't know
what we should have done without them. It
was a curious sight to see this one spot illuminated as bright as day, while all around was
inky darkness; the Egyptian soldiers, in their
white uniform and red fezes, puddling about
ankle-deep in water as they toiled along with

the heavy tins or pumped away standing up on
the tops of the great storage tanks.   There was
little to break the silence but the sucking of the
pumps, or perhaps a loud remark from one or
other of us, more often the reverse of parliamen-
tary, addressed to some of the fatigue party.
Every now and then the engine would give a
whistle as it started with its heavy load slowly
along the line in the darkness.   The engine-
driver fell asleep at last from sheer exhaustion,
so I, by way of a little relaxation, manned the
engine and drove the train up and down the
line.   In this way the night wore on till at length
we had filled the last mussock.

Then we joined the camels and woke up the
drivers, who were sleeping on the ground rolled
in their blankets.   There were one or two
officers with the various detachments of camels
making up the whole number, and these soon
had their men together and ready to load up ;
so we dismissed the Egyptians and went to work
at once to get the tins on the camels, for it
was now nearly three o'clock in the morning, and
we should have to march in an hour and a half.

As each section of fifty camels was loaded we
marched them off with orders to halt opposite
the Head-quarter camp.

During this time we were working by the electric light thrown on us from the *Dolphin*, which gave a curious weird appearance to the mass of men in their many-coloured garments as they toiled away with a will to get the seven hundred camels loaded before the day should begin to break. Affghans, Soumalis, Punjabis, and Bengalis, all mixed up together, toiled on through the remainder of the night, and the camels grunted and groaned and made the hours hideous with their horrible sounds.

Each camel had two tins or two barrels put on him, so they had an easy load. The Indian camels moved along in strings of three, but the Berbera animals were not tied, a driver looking after three or four of them. Some of the barrels leaked very much, as the wood had become very dry, and the mussocks, as I have already said, very soon parted with half their contents. The last section was loaded as the sky began to blush in the east with the presage of the early dawn, and we had still half an hour left us before the day would break. What a night of toil it had been! and what an age it seemed since one o'clock the previous afternoon! Hot, tired, sleepless, and foodless, we had still only half completed our task as yet, and we had still

before us many hours of work, of marching, and
probably of fighting, in all the heat of the noonday sun.

It will be long indeed before I forget the
kindness of a friend who brought me a cup of
cocoa as I was mounting my horse to catch up
the front line of camels. It is always thus with
soldiers—those who have give to those that
have not, though the one may be an entire
stranger to the other, and though they meet
them for the first time, and never perhaps afterwards. It is this *cameraderie* among members
of the same cloth which marks the English
soldier above all others, and makes the English
army what it is. I have seen men almost
starving, yet share with a comrade what would
hardly fill their own mouths three times over ;
and I have noticed others parched with thirst
themselves offer, it may be to a stranger, the
cup of precious water before they put it to
their own lips. It is in trying circumstances, in
times of tribulation, and, above all, in times of
war, that the noblest qualities of a man are
brought out, and that a spirit unknown before
shines at length brilliant in its true colours.

But we had to push forward ; the different
units of the force were gathering together and

forming up into three sides of one vast square, in the middle of which were hundreds of camels, our water detachment being but a quarter of the gathering,—mules drawing carts with entrenching tools, teams of horses, ambulances, dhoolies with their bearers ready to receive their ghastly burdens, and the various detachments of the field hospitals with their doctors and appliances. The cavalry were already out in front; the sun was just rising above the horizon, and in a few minutes his heat would reach us, when at length the vast concourse of men and baggage-animals began to move, and the advance had begun. The huge square, measuring some eight hundred yards across, went forward in a cloud of dust without hurry and without noise, save the clank of arms, and with all that marvellous precision of movement attained by perfect organization and thorough training, for around us was some of the flower of the British army—a chosen force, perfect in every detail, animated by one spirit, ready for any emergency.

So forward we went in all the

" Pride, pomp, and circumstance of glorious war "

and the advance had begun at last.

CHAPTER VII.

HASHEEN.

THE troops composing the great square, in which
formation we advanced towards Hasheen, were
as follows :—The front face was composed of
three battalions of the 2nd Brigade, viz. the 49th,
70th, and Royal Marines ; the other regiment of
this brigade, the 53rd, having been left behind
to look after the camp.   On the right face were
the Brigade of Guards, and the left face was
formed by the Indian Brigade, viz. the 15th
Sikhs and the 17th and 28th Bombay Native
Infantry.   The troops inside the square, besides
the Commissariat and Transport Corps, were
the 17th and 24th companies of the Royal
Engineers, some Madras Sappers and Miners,
two rocket-troughs of the Royal Artillery and
a battery of Gardner guns.   The cavalry force
in front was composed of two squadrons of the
5th Lancers, two squadrons of the 20th Hussars,

and four squadrons of the 9th Bengal Cavalry.
There was also in front a battery of Royal
Horse Artillery and the greater part of the
Mounted Infantry.

With the cavalry and mounted infantry covering the front we marched along through the
bush, which in this part is somewhat scanty, and
did not impede us much. The square moved
a little too fast for the baggage-animals, and
there being no rear face to it, there was a good
deal of straggling in spite of all endeavours to
push the camels along. It was a perpetual
drive, drive, drive; but very few loads were
displaced, and none of the water was lost except
through the leaking of the barrels and the skins.

So, with the sun scorching on our backs, we
marched along till we lost sight of Suakin, and
at length, without opposition, reached the isolated hills to which I referred in the last
chapter.

It was now about half-past eight, and we had
come a distance of six miles or more. The
square was halted for a few minutes, while our
generals scanned the hills and mountains in front
and settled their plan of attack, as it was seen
that the enemy did not mean us to have it all
our own way as we had had the day before, and

that since yesterday he had concentrated his forces and was fully intending to oppose our further advance. The country in front of us was covered with a dense, thorny bush ; there were a few rough tracks here and there, but for the most part it was entirely overgrown. Nearer the hills the bush was much higher, quite high enough indeed to hide a man on a horse, but the hills themselves were bare and rugged, and very precipitous.

One large isolated hill, a thousand feet high and a mile and a half long, stood like a great island out of the surrounding bush, and on the other side of this hill was the village of Hasheen. On the right, and three-quarters of a mile from Hasheen Hill, were the mountains, some two or three thousand feet high, which here abut on to the plain, and then turn again in a north-easterly direction towards Handoub, distant from here seven miles. Behind Hasheen the range of mountains trends away in a north-westerly direction till they circle round to where the village of Tamai is situated, twelve miles to the south-west.

In front of where we halted stood two conical-shaped hills, one behind the other, and two hundred feet in height, while to the left of this

there was a much lower hill, which was afterwards used as the point where the General
Commanding took his stand. These hills were
to the south of Hasheen Hill, and a mile from
it, and were not occupied by the enemy. The
70th Regiment and the convoys were ordered
off to take up their position between the two
conical hills above mentioned, and to construct
a zariba connecting them together. Sand-bag
redoubts were to be at once thrown up on the
summit of each, to hold two guns of the Horse
Artillery battery, and the Royal Engineers and
Madras Sappers were soon at work dragging
the heavy pieces of timber they had brought
with them up the steep sides.

In the meanwhile the 49th, supported by half
a battalion of Marines, was ordered to take
the great hill in front which I have called
Hasheen Hill. They went forward, and very
soon were advancing steadily up the precipitous
slopes under a heavy fire from the enemy, who
were posted at the very summit. Never hesi-
tating an instant, they continued to ascend the
hill, neither pausing to get breath nor waiting
to return the enemy's fire till they reached a
kind of ledge half-way up. Then they opened
on the Arabs, and the rattle of the musketry

echoed round the adjoining mountains as volley after volley was poured in. A few moments only, and then again the gallant 49th pressed forward, carrying out their advance as if at some parade at home. Steadily they ascended the steep rocky ground in front of them, while the enemy, almost invisible behind the boulders and rocks, redoubled their fire, and sought, if possible, to stem the tide sweeping towards them. But it was no good ; the firing at the summit began to grow weaker and weaker, as the 49th and the Marines got nearer to it ; and then a few minutes more and the hill was crowned, and a heavy fire at once opened upon the retreating Arabs. Wreaths of smoke wrapped the top of Hasheen Hill, and told that in this part of the field our troops had gallantly carried out the work given them to do.

A more splendidly executed movement could never have been witnessed ; it was simply magnificent, and called forth the praise of all who saw it. After a long march, in a burning sun and under a heavy fire, the men moved as if on parade, taking advantage of every bit of cover the ground afforded, and going steadily to their work in a manner that defied all opposition.

While this was going on on the left, the

other half-battalion of the Royal Marines was advancing up the ravine formed by the mountains on the right and Hasheen Hill on the left. The bush in this part was densely thick, and it was not without considerable difficulty that they were able to march through it. The half-battalion moved in column of companies ready at any moment to form into square. In front of them the Mounted Infantry were at work driving back bodies of the enemy who kept rushing towards them, till stopped by a volley or two, and then retiring again to renew the same tactics.

The 20th Hussars were operating on the left, while the 9th Bengal Cavalry, with the 5th Lancers, were on the right. The bush was so thick that it was absolutely impossible for cavalry to act with any effect, and I much doubt whether they ought ever to have been used, as they were, in such a country. A squadron of the 9th were advancing by troops on the right flank, when they suddenly found themselves in the midst of a strong body of the enemy. Unable to charge, they simply were ordered to the right-about, and retired at a gallop to get out of the ambush into which they had fallen. In a certain amount of disorder

L

they fell back, and as they galloped to the rear
to reform as rapidly as possible, they were
simply run down by the Arabs. With surpris-
ing agility these fellows sped over the ground
after the retreating horsemen, seeming almost
to fly through the bush as they sprang from
place to place. Rushing up behind the horses,
they would hamstring the poor animals, and thus
bring the riders to the ground. There was no
time to stop and help those who were in this
way dismounted, as the men, owing to the
thickness of the bush, were much scattered.
They had to fight as best they could, and fall
and die when they were outnumbered by the
rush of Arabs. Three Arabs attacked one of
the dismounted men, who fought hard indeed
for his life. Spearing one, and cutting down
another with his sword, he was preparing to
despatch his third antagonist, when he was
himself run through from behind, and thus fell
without a friendly arm to help him. The 5th
Lancers had been halted in a somewhat open
piece of ground to the left of where this
was going on, and waiting his opportunity,
their commander, with considerable forethought,
delivered his charge on the flank of the pursuing
Arabs, going right through them, and then

wheeling round and taking them again as he returned to his starting-point to reform. The Arabs practised their usual tactics, and lay themselves flat on the ground when they saw the cavalry approaching, doing their best to hamstring the horses as they passed, but the lance put an end to many of these thus sacrificed to their temerity. The leader of this little charge, who was a true soldier and thorough type of a dashing cavalry officer, was himself wounded by one of the spears of the 9th, with which an Arab had armed himself. Kneeling on the ground, the fellow kept himself in front of the officer, who was thus rather perplexed to know what he was going to do, so he went straight for him with his drawn sword. The Arab suddenly jumped on one side, and as the horseman passed him, endeavoured to run him through with the lance. So quick was the Arab that the sword was too late to parry the thrust, and the spear was lodged deeply in the rider's thigh, so deeply indeed as to wrench it from the Arab's grasp. With the bridle in one hand and a sword in the other, there was no possibility of withdrawing the lance, which caught in a bush and nearly unhorsed this gallant soldier. The enemy lost a good few men in this part of the

field, and another officer belonging to the 5th
Lancers laid four of the enemy low before he
emptied his revolver. It was proved again that
a sword against a spear and a shield is absolutely useless, and that a lance is the only
weapon of offence in this sort of warfare. In a
fairly open piece of ground a regiment of Lancers
would simply annihilate any force of Arabs
opposed to them ; and if it ever comes again to
our having to do battle with this magnificent
and warlike race, a complete regiment of Lancers
should be sent out, and not two squadrons of a
regiment in one case, and a regiment unused to
the lance in another.

But there was busy work going on in other
parts of the field.

A large party of the enemy, some fifteen
hundred strong, had made a circuitous march
round our right flank, and quite unperceived,
suddenly appeared in our rear between us and
Suakin, evidently with the intention of cutting
off our retreat in the event of their force in front
being successful. But the gunners, who by this
time had dragged one of their guns into position
on the top of each of the two conical hills,
viewed them before they were able to get
within a thousand yards of us, and within a very

few seconds were plunging shell into the middle of them, when they immediately scattered through the bush and made their way back again to where they started from. Artillery has a great moral effect upon the Arabs, and they have a wholesome horror of the " big guns."

About this time news was brought in that large bodies of the enemy were pouring over from the direction of Tamai and threatening our left flank, so the Indian infantry, who before this were stationed in the valley, formed in three sides of a square, were now moved off in this direction and deployed into line. Probably the movement was seen by the enemy, who swung round to the rear of Hasheen Hill and were lost to sight.

The Guards had been ordered to advance up the valley as a support to the 2nd Brigade, and in a huge square they were forcing their way through the dense bush. The Coldstreams formed the front face of this square, four companies of the Scots were on each of the two side faces, and the Grenadiers made the rear face, while a battery of Gardner guns, manned by the Marine Artillery, also accompanied the square. In this formation they were thrown forward, and when they had advanced about a mile were

halted with the dense bush all round them. Of
course it was impossible for them to retain their
formation intact, and the different faces were
broken here and there by patches of the thorny
jungle. From their position they could see
nothing of the enemy for some time, though
bullets were whistling over their heads in considerable numbers, evidently fired from the
mountains, where the enemy were in great force.
A party of six hundred Arabs all of a sudden
appeared on the right face of the square, and
with the utmost ferocity charged down upon it ;
but the Guards, standing as steady as a wall,
received them with a withering volley, which
stretched half their number lifeless on the sand.
Supported by a large force some three thousand
strong, this party renewed their fruitless efforts,
and, led in their charges by a youth mounted
on a white camel, did their utmost to gain the
mastery ; but it was utterly useless, for they had
opposed to them some of the finest troops in the
world.

The roar of the musketry was now general
over the whole field, the enemy were firing away
in the valley and along the lower ridges of the
mountains where the mounted infantry were
driving them back, the 49th and the Marines

were showering bullets down from their point of vantage, while the rattle of the musketry in the bush in front told of the Guards being hotly engaged. Volley succeeded volley, and amidst the crack, crack, of the rifles, the booming of the guns re-echoed through the mountains, as the Horse Artillery pitched their shells with unerring precision into the enemy wherever he showed thickest and in the greatest numbers.

Another determined attack was made on our right flank, where the 70th were hard at work under a covering party building the zariba ; but these fellows being charged by the 5th Lancers and 9th Bengal Cavalry, were driven off and great numbers of them killed.

A little before one o'clock, the enemy's fire having slackened, the 49th and Marines were withdrawn from Hasheen Hill and ordered to fall back towards the conical hills in rear. The Guards were also ordered to retire.

No sooner had the 49th and Marines begun to descend their hill, than the top was almost instantaneously re-occupied by the enemy, who opened a brisk fire on our retiring troops. A large force also having ascended the lower part of this hill where it rose out of the valley, opened an exceedingly heavy fire on the Brigade

of Guards now also falling back. Their square
was much hampered by being absolutely filled
with baggage-animals, dhoolie-bearers, cavalry,
and even artillery, who had all taken refuge
inside it, to escape from the effects of the
Guards' heavy fire. There was no hurry, and
the men moved with the utmost steadiness
under the galling fire poured in upon them.
Every now and then the square would halt
and reply with a volley or two ; but they were
unable to see the crafty enemy, who took good
care to hide himself behind the thickest of the
bush, and the rocky ground of the hills. Many
a man fell, shot dead, and many were hit ;
while more than one officer fell, mortally
wounded, inside the square. The dead and
wounded alike were all placed inside the dhoolies, and this caused a certain amount of delay,
as parts of the force were halted to look after
the casualties. Falling back in this way was a
slow, tedious business, and it has never been
revealed why the Guards were ever put forward
into an impenetrable jungle to stand and be
shot at. Under the most disadvantageous circumstances they behaved with the utmost coolness, and the majestic way in which they carried
out their retreat, over about a mile and a half

of the roughest country, beset by an invisible enemy, is deserving of the highest praise. It is not too much to say that had the enemy been better marksmen, and understood thoroughly the use of their rifles, the Brigade of Guards would have been simply decimated. It was folly first of all to put them in such a position, but this folly was surpassed by the way the retreat was ordered. By the falling back of the 49th and Marines from Hasheen Hill, we gave back to the enemy a position for which our men had fought most gallantly, and from which they were able to annoy us considerably without our being in any way able to reply. With no means of covering their retreat, and with a considerable part of the cavalry actually inside their square, the Guards were exposed for an hour or more to a fire, which, if it had been better directed, would have nearly annihilated them. To run such risks is hardly forethought, and to handle troops thus is not generalship.

With the falling back of the Brigade of Guards and the two battalions of the 2nd Brigade, the firing ceased along the whole line, and the action was virtually over.

There was a report that the enemy was threatening our left flank, and that large bodies were advancing from that direction ; but this was found to be groundless, and moreover, there was force enough in that part of the field to repel any attack, as we could just see the Indian Brigade still standing there in line, while their forms seemed to dance in the mirage of the intense heat.

The formation of the force, after the various battalions had fallen back, was as follows. The right was protected by the two hills, and the zariba, now almost completed, and held by the 70th. Next to this the remaining four guns of the Horse Artillery battery took up a position on the low hill to the left, which I have already referred to as being the point where the Staff were stationed. In rear of this was a part of the cavalry. Further to the left were the three battalions of the Guards, and the 49th and Royal Marines ; while on the left flank were the Indian battalions drawn up in line at right angles to the remainder of the troops, and in rear of them. The general formation was thus three sides of a square.

Bodies of the enemy were to be seen hovering about the base of the mountains, and on these the artillery opened fire for upwards of twenty minutes. Many of the shells took effect, but the range was a very long one, and it was extremely difficult to see in what measure our fire was successful. No further attempt was made by the Arabs to attack us, and so the men were allowed to sit down and eat their dinners, while the wounded were brought in to t he field hospitals and the dead collected and laid carefully in the dhoolies. The doctors had their hands pretty full, and they had to attend to ghastly wounds, for the spears cut long and deep. I am sure nobody will deny the doctors a word of praise for their devotion and self-sacrifice, and for their kindness and gentleness to the suffering. Present in the very forefront of the action all through the day, they were always at the point where they were most wanted, and many were the cases where lives were saved through their prompt attention which otherwise must have been most assuredly lost. One at least met his death when engaged in this work of mercy, and grand as the death is of a man who falls fighting for Queen and Country, that of one who yields up his life while tending the poor suffering mortals around him on the battle-field seems to me not one whit less glorious.

The water transport had now plenty to do

serving out water to the different regiments.
Half a gallon was allowed per man, and camels
were sent off in all directions carrying the re-
freshment the men so much needed. We had
brought out with the force nearly twelve
thousand gallons of water, so that there was not
only plenty for every one, but sufficient to give
the horses and mules a drink, though I am afraid
from this not being generally known a good
many animals went without. The camels had
been watered the night before, so they required
none.

The zariba was being rapidly strengthened,
and a portion of the battery of Gardner guns
was also being posted inside it, so with the 70th
to hold the zariba, and the two hills armed with
a gun each, the place seemed sufficiently strong
to hold out against any odds. Provisions for
four days for this force had been brought out,
and nearly six thousand gallons of water was
stored partly in three large iron tanks and a
canvas tank which the Engineers had carried
out with them. There was also a considerable
store of ammunition, so altogether the zariba
was well found. The zariba was a small one,
the two conical-shaped hills being connected
by two high hedges made out of the thorny

bush running parallel to each other, and about thirty yards apart. A shallow trench was dug in rear of this hedge, and the sand thrown up against the hedge to give it additional strength. Sentries were placed all along the trench at night time, and the men always slept in such a position that they were ready at any moment to defend different portions of the work. The distance across from the top of one hill to the top of the other was not more than one hundred and fifty yards. A signalling-party was also posted on one of the hills, so that communication might in this way be kept up with Suakin by means of the heliograph.

At half past three o'clock the artillery ceased firing, and there were no further signs of the enemy to be seen. The men were by this time rested, and orders were accordingly given to prepare to march back again to Suakin. It was some time before all was ready, as the various battalions had to be marched into position, and the camels and mules collected before a start could be made for home.

The formation in which our return march was made was the same as that in which we had advanced in the morning. The Guards were on the proper right, marching in column of companies, the Indian Brigade was on the left, while the two battalions of the 2nd Brigade formed the rear or proper front face. In the inside of the square were the transport animals, and the dhoolies, and dhoolie-bearers carrying our killed and our wounded.

I believe all our killed were brought in and buried the following day at the Christian Cemetery down by the harbour. The wounded were taken to the base hospital, and afterwards transferred to the *Ganges* hospital-ship.

Our losses were officially returned as follows : three officers and twenty non-commissioned officers and men killed, and two officers and forty-one non-commissioned officers and men wounded.

There were several cases of sunstroke and extreme exhaustion, but this is not to be wondered at as the men had been under arms since before four o'clock in the morning, and every one had had a hard day's work. The march out to Hasheen was a hot and tedious one of over seven miles, then followed the fight and heavy work of the day in a sun which absolutely seemed to singe, and when all this was over there was the march home again through the prickly bush and heavy sand. The whole force worked magnificently and the General ought to have been proud of his troops. They deserved all the praise they got. The honour of the day no doubt belonged to the 49th and the Marines, whose feat of the morning will long remain in our memories ; but all alike deserved praise, though some had a better chance of distinguishing themselves than others.

A good many of us were much struck with the tactics of the enemy, who worked on a regular system and evidently a prearranged plan.

First of all they relinquished the two conical hills to us, and fell back to the superior range in rear, from which they had complete command of the whole ground in front.

Their tactics in the valley were, no doubt, intended to draw us on, as they purposely concealed their main body in the hollow behind Hasheen Hill. In this way a smaller force continued to retire slowly before the half battalion of Marines and the Native Infantry, always just retaining touch and keeping up all the while a tolerably brisk fire. But the officer commanding the Royal Marines, who was an experienced soldier of many a hard-fought field, told me himself that he saw through their little game and halted his half-battalion to await orders.

While they engaged us in the front in this way, they managed to lay in wait for our cavalry, a part of whom they entrapped, while with a considerable force they threatened our right and left flanks simultaneously, and despatched as well a body, fifteen hundred strong, to attack us in rear. Had it not been for the guns of the Horse Artillery on the hills, there is no doubt that this attempt on our rear would have been successful, and the whole of our transport destroyed.

The transport was huddled together on the left of the zariba, and without any guard except two companies of the 70th, all the other men being hard at work building the zariba. I was told by an officer, who was stationed here all the day, that when he was ordered to get his men together to protect the transport from an attack, which at that moment seemed imminent, he only had sufficient men to put along one side of the mass of animals, and those were a yard apart— an efficient defence this against the impetuous onslaught of a large force of Arabs!

Altogether the generalship on the part of the enemy was good, and it was lucky for us we went out as strong as we did. Most of the men we engaged were of the Hadendowa tribes, but

we heard afterwards, that a large force of some
three thousand Amarars were drawn up in
rear, waiting to see which way the fight went—
so much for the " friendlies."

The strength of the enemy was variously
estimated at from eight to twelve thousand men,
but reports differed materially in different parts
of the field. The intense thickness of the bush
prevented our seeing what their strength really
was, and, added to this, there were large bodies
of men in the mountains watching their opportunity. I do not think myself there were as
many as ten thousand men present, but I had
no opportunity of seeing what the strength of
the party was that came over from the Tamai
direction. Their losses must have been very
heavy, for added to the execution done by the
Mounted Infantry and the Cavalry, the 49th and
Marines must have slain a considerable number;
and further than this the steady and very heavy
fire of the Guards' square must have told considerably on the dense formation, in which the
enemy made their repeated charges. The
artillery fire was also not without effect. The
opinion among many was that there must have
been twelve hundred of the Arabs killed; but I
should fancy a thousand would be nearer the

M

mark. To this must be added the number of
wounded, which must of necessity have been
considerable also.

With our own wounded brought back to
camp, was the youth who led the charges on the
Guards' square, riding on a white camel. He
was slightly wounded and made a prisoner of,
being afterwards taken to the " H " Redoubt
Hospital, where he received every care and
attention, just as one of our own men. I don't
know whether he appreciated a cot provided
with sheets, which must have been a somewhat
foreign luxury to him, but he was kept in a
tent by himself, and had a man continually
watching him, both for his own sake as well as
for other reasons. His great grief was that his
white camel had been killed, and he seemed to
find it a hard matter to get over this. I do not
think he ever showed any particular signs of
gratitude for the kindnesses he received; but this
was hardly to be expected from a representative
of the race, who hated and detested us most
bitterly.

I alluded just now to the way in which the
transport animals were left without any efficient
guard to look over them. The English portion
of the transport was of course not numerous

enough to be of any use, added to which they had their work cut out for them to look after the native drivers. A part of the Transport Corps was, moreover, told off to occupy the small hill on the left, which duty should surely have been carried out by some one else, and thus the chance of guarding or defending the camels was reduced to a minimum.

There was another thing at which we were somewhat astonished, and that was that the transport, comprising in all, that day, somewhere about twelve hundred camels, was suffered to march the whole way out from Suakin to where the force made their first halt, a mile from the conical hills, without any guard whatsoever. We have often wondered since how it was the enemy did not take advantage of this, as he might so easily have done by one of his rapidly executed movements.

Many hours were not, however, destined to pass before a fearful fate was to overtake this same transport through the laxity and carelessness on the part of those responsible for its protection, and through an overweening confidence in their own strength.

Our march back was a long business and a very tedious one, for we were all thoroughly tired. A hot sun scorched our backs and the dust half suffocated us, but the camp came into sight at last, with Suakin behind it in the distance, and in another hour we were passing the line of redoubts and the different battalions were breaking off to their own parts of the camp, while those we had left behind came out to meet us to hear the news or to assure themselves of the safety of some friend.

We rode on down to the Head-quarter camp to make our report, and then, just as the sun set, we reached our own tents, having had a spell of work of over thirty hours with little or no food and without a rest of any kind. We were almost too tired to eat, and sleep was all we asked for ; but our night was not without alarms, and many shots were fired. I think, though, it would have taken heavy firing indeed to have disturbed some of us.

Our first real fight with the Hadendowas was thus over, though what was gained by it nobody ever knew. The enemy on their side celebrated it as a victory, while her Gracious Majesty on ours sent a telegram congratulating the troops on their success and thanking them for their gallantry.

All that was gained by the action of Hasheen

was the possession of two small hills which we
secured without firing a shot, and before the
fighting began. It was generally supposed that
we marched out with the intention of occupying
Hasheen, and of thus depriving the enemy of
their water supply in this part of the country;
but we never went within a mile of the wells,
which had been noticed by the reconnoitring
party the day before, and we contented ourselves
with leaving a force behind in a barren situation,
too small in itself to take any active measures
against the enemy, and depending the whole
while they stopped there on their friends at
Suakin being able to run them out convoys of
supplies and water.

To the Arab mind a defeat is not a defeat
unless the one force can follow up his advantage
and drive home his blow. No wonder, then,
that when they saw us retire from the positions
we had carried in the morning, and then quietly
march off back again to camp in the afternoon,
they concluded we had had the worst of it, and
agreed to celebrate the affair as a victory. The
mere killing of a certain number of their force
means nothing at all to them, and unless they
are dispersed, shattered, and absolutely driven
off the field, it is as much their victory as that

of their enemies, and most certainly they do not reckon it a defeat.

As to the moral effect the battle of Hasheen had upon them, this was illustrated two days after, and showed in an unmistakable way that it amounted to *nil*.

How far our generals were justified in their course it is neither my wish nor my intention to inquire. We in the force only knew that many good men and true fell that day, and we knew also that as soldiers we had done what we were ordered, and done it to the best of our ability ; but how far the blood then shed helped us on our way at all, or furthered the object of the campaign, we were at a loss to imagine, and were never afterwards enlightened.

CHAPTER VIII.

THE ZARIBA.

As I said in the last chapter, many of us enjoyed
a fair night's sleep, and by four o'clock the next
morning we were ready for more work, and
more fighting if necessary. When I talk of a
night's rest, though, I do not mean that we went
to bed comfortably, for we none of us took our
clothes off, but merely lay down as we were, with
our loaded revolvers and our swords beside us,
too dead tired for anything else.

I must mention an amusing little episode to
do with the way we carried out our ablutions.
A few days before we had "come by" a barrel
of water, which we annexed for the purpose of
having a good bath. We then secured the half
of an old water-butt, and filling it nearly full of
water, proceeded solemnly to take a tub in it
one after the other, and five of us thus enjoyed
the first real wash we had had for a very long

time. We did not upset the water, though, after our first wash, but kept it religiously, and for the next five days continued to tub in it whenever we had a chance. By the morning after we returned from the battle of Hasheen we had been separated from our tub for two days, and when it came to the first one's turn to wash, I saw him at work with an iron cup, skimming a thick glutinous scum from the top of the water, after completing which operation, with the utmost gravity, he as solemnly proceeded to take his tub like a true Englishman. I must confess that the black and putrescent water of our bath that morning defeated me, and I never tubbed again.

It was evident that another advance was contemplated almost immediately, and though no orders were issued about where we were going to march to next, we, in the afternoon of the 21st of March, were told that we were to have as much water as possible loaded up and ready to start an hour before daybreak on the next morning.

Owing to the number of tins we had left at the Hasheen Zariba, we were rather short of means of carrying a large supply of water, but all through that night we worked on again

pretty much in the same way as we had done
two nights before, and filled every vessel we
could get hold of. By four o'clock we were
marching off to join the remainder of the Transport up at the Right Water Fort, where also the
whole of the troops were paraded before starting.

The force which marched out this Sunday
morning, the 22nd of March, was composed as
follows : The 49th, the Royal Marines, the
Indian Brigade, a battery of four Gardner guns,
a detachment of the Royal Engineers, and a
squadron of the 5th Lancers, and 9th Bengal
Cavalry. There was, of course, as well a proper
complement of dhoolie-bearers, doctors, and
ambulances, an ammunition column, a telegraph-
cart, with wires, etc., and a huge number of
transport animals carrying supplies for four
thousand men for three days.

We were all on the move by half-past four
o'clock. In front, the 49th and Marines, with
the battery of Gardner guns, moved in one
square, while in rear was a second square composed of the Indian Infantry, with the whole of
the transport.

The orders were that this force was to advance
about five or six miles in the direction of Tamai;
that is south-south-west of Suakin, and there

halt and build a zariba, in which the stores and water were to be left, guarded by a portion of the force, while the remainder were to return to the camp with the transport animals as soon as the work had been accomplished. In this way a kind of depôt was to be formed well on the way to Tamai, and stores of all sorts were to be massed there by convoys marching out daily from Suakin.

The whole of the force was under command of General MacNeill, and the advance was undisturbed by the enemy, who indeed showed no signs of being anywhere in the neighbourhood. The first part of the march was through country covered with small isolated patches of bush, but nothing to impede the advance of the troops. Further on, the bush became much thicker and closer, and the cavalry had some difficulty in forcing their way through it, being thus prevented from obtaining a thorough view of the surrounding ground.

Having arrived at length at a point about six miles out, the whole force was halted and three zaribas marked out, joining one another, and placed like the squares on a chess-board taken diagonally. The two outside squares were occupied by the 49th and Marines, having two

Gardner guns in each, while the third or centre square, which was double the size of the other two, was occupied by the Indian Brigade, and was the one in which all the stores were placed.

After a short interval for rest, a part of the force was ordered to pile their arms and set to work at once to cut down the bush and drag it in to build the zariba, while others were digging trenches or helping to unload the transport animals and carry the cases of tinned meat and biscuits into the centre square. Later on the men were allowed to sit down and have their dinners, for they wanted a little rest, as the march had been a heavy one, and the work of cutting down and dragging the bush about was exceedingly hard in the intense heat of the sun.

The men were thus for the most part much scattered about. Two companies of the 49th were out some forty yards away from their zariba, their arms lying down on the ground, while they hacked and hewed at the tough growth of the bush. The Marines were similarly en-gaged, and the Indian Infantry were hard at work on their zariba as well. The greater part of the transport animals had been unladen, and the stores placed in the centre of the large

square. The camels were drawn up in a body
on one side of, and about seventy yards from,
the zaribas of the Marines and the Indian
Brigade. A few cavalry videttes were out in
the bush, but few of these were more than thirty
yards away from the working parties.

All around seemed quiet; the men continued
at their work, and the two small sandbag redoubts at the corners of the zaribas of the 49th
and Marines were gradually being completed,
when a cavalry vidette came galloping in to tell
the General that parties of the enemy had been
seen not far off in the bush. The General was
asking the man in what force he thought the
enemy were, when a second vidette came in
telling the same story, that the Arabs were collecting in force round the zaribas. Then suddenly the air was rent with the most frightful
yell; the cavalry outposts came clattering in,
dashing through the working parties, and a heavy
fire was poured upon us from the enemy, who
seemed all at once to have sprung out of the
earth where but a second before all had seemed
so quiet and so still. There was a cry all round,
" Stand to your arms, men !" " Stand to your
arms !" but, alas! many of the men were without
arms, for they had put them down on the ground

while they were toiling away at their work. There was a rush to the partially formed zaribas, and, mixed up together, Englishmen and Indians stood back to back fighting for life against an overwhelming force.

A large body of the Arabs had at the same time attacked the mass of camels and transport animals, who turned round and, like a vast surging sea, came onward towards the zaribas, crashing through the bush, swaying with their mighty weight, and trampling down everything in their course as they swept forward enveloped in a dense cloud of dust, maddened and terrified. The Arabs were among them, hacking, hewing right and left, ham-stringing and ripping up the wretched camels, and cutting down mercilessly the poor miserable native drivers who, unarmed and helpless, were hemmed in and carried onward by the flood. Many of our own men and officers, too, were in this way driven forward, unable to extricate themselves or even to draw their swords. Mules, horses, and camels were huddled into one hopeless mass of inextricable confusion, while the air was filled with the screams of men and animals and the roar of the musketry.

The 17th Native Infantry had possession of

this side of the centre zariba, the Marines being
on their left. It was on this point that the con-
fused mass of men and animals fell. The 17th
were for the moment completely scattered, but
groups of men stood fast here and there, and
poured in their fire, in the general confusion,
right into the men and animals in front of them.
It was a minute before they were able to form
up in any way, and then they fired upon friend
and foe at once, and men and animals went down
before the leaden hail, killed by our own bullets.
But the Marines on the left stood firm as a
rock, and it was well they did. The enemy
dashed onwards, with almost irresistible impulse,
falling in terrible numbers before their well-
directed volleys, and not being stopped until
they were actually touching our bayonets. Led
by sheikhs carrying white banners inscribed
with the Mahdi's name, they charged again and
again, rushing up to the face of the square and
engaging our men hand-to-hand. Many of
these Arabs would fall before the rain of bullets,
but, picking themselves up instantly, they would
dash forward with the rest, till, pierced through
and through, they reached the square at last, posi-
tively riddled by the fire. It was a supremely
awful moment, but the English foot-soldier again

proved himself invincible, and stood facing the foe—which outnumbered him ten to one—without a waver and without a move, save to load and reload or drive home the thrust of the weapon in the use of which he ranks before all others. So Arab and Englishman hacked and hewed, and shot and thrust, till blood flowed out on the ground like water, and black and white man alike bit the dust or writhed in death-agony on the hot sands of that parched-up desert.

The 49th zariba was entered by about a hundred and fifty Arabs, as most of the men were, as I have already said, outside, cutting down the bush. Getting their arms as quickly as possible, two companies of this gallant regiment formed rallying squares, and in this formation none of the Arabs could touch them. They did their best with shot and spear alike, led on, as in other parts of the field, by sheikhs carrying banners, on one of which was inscribed the words in Arabic, "Whosoever fights under this banner shall have victory." So crafty were the enemy in the way they attacked these detached portions of our force, that they got round between them and the zaribas, as they saw that our men would not be able to fire in this direction for fear of

injuring their friends.   But cold steel did what
the bullet was unable to do.

Nothing could have exceeded the coolness
and signal bravery of the 49th, as they fought
their zariba against overwhelming numbers, who
never faltered for a moment in delivering charge
upon charge.   It was the triumph of perfect
discipline, combined with the utmost bravery,
over a glorious pluck untutored in the ways of
war.   Nothing but this saved our force that day.
Had there been the least unsteadiness, had there
been the slightest hesitation on our side, our
force must have been doomed.   Nothing could
have saved us but this perfect self-possession and
steadiness when taken at a disadvantage.   Had
it not been for the sterling quality of the English troops, another catastrophe more awful than
that of Isandlanha, another massacre more fearful than that of Maiwand, must have occurred
that Sunday afternoon.   Never did the sterling
quality of the British soldier shine out more
brightly than it did on this occasion.   Never did
men face death more resolutely and with greater
sang-froid.   The glory of the British army has
not yet departed, when deeds of this sort can be
performed.   Happy is the country who possesses
such soldiers ; the people of England ought to be

proud of them, and a General ought to be thankful indeed who has such men at his back to pull him through.

But I must go back. The remainder of the 49th were in an incredible short space of time in position, and a hand-to-hand fight with the Arabs who had entered their square ensued. Some were shot down, while others were run through with the bayonet, till, fighting splendidly, the last of these fanatical and undaunted warriors fell, a victim to his indomitable pluck. One hundred and twenty-two bodies of Arabs were counted actually inside the square after the fight was over, and among them, strewed pretty thickly, were many of our own men, soldier and sailor alike. The Gardner guns had opened on the enemy and swept the ground in front, carrying death and destruction wherever they were pointed, but they became jammed almost immediately, and then the enemy were among the sailors in a second ; a few only escaped being wounded, while many, alas ! were killed. They fought their guns gloriously, and fell, as British sailors have done before, side by side with their soldier-brothers.

The redoubt in the zariba furthest from Suakin was the scene of some of the most severe

N

hand-to-hand fighting ; and it was here the sailors suffered most, no less than one officer and ten blue-jackets, who had been working the guns, lying here dead in a heap.

I ought to mention an incident of the fight, showing how the enemy are animated by a bitter hatred for us, and how this hatred is not confined to the Arab men alone, but fills the hearts of their women and their children also. For one single instant the smoke cleared off and showed us the swarming hordes of Arabs leaping and dancing in the bush, while they rushed onward in endless numbers to demolish us if possible ; and as we thus gained a momentary view, there stood out between the two opposing forces a boy, aged not more than twelve years, without signs of fear, actually throwing stones at us. But the Arab fire was growing hot, ours opened again, and the fate of that boy was sealed, not because there was the slightest wish on the part of our men to slay the little fellow, but because one and all were hopelessly doomed before that terrific and deadly hail. There were women, too, fighting like the men, and dressed in the Mahdi's uniform. It was horrible to think of their being there, and worse still to think that they had to fall. But there was no help for it ; in the short half-hour that the fight lasted there was no time to pick and choose, and though we never knew till afterwards that there were women in the enemy's ranks, the dead bodies of several lying on the field told more surely than anything else of the bitter enmity there was between us.

The enemy did not, however, confine their attacks to one side of the zaribas alone ; they were on all sides, and the Sikhs and 28th had a hot time of it. The Sikhs especially behaved most gallantly, magnificent fellows that they are. They were perfectly in hand the whole while, and stood as firm as rocks, carrying out the orders of their officers and plying their bayonets with the utmost effect. Many Arabs had entered this zariba ; and indeed some were seen quietly to trot across it before we were hardly aware that we were attacked. These fellows actually succeeded in running up behind some of our men and in stabbing them while they were still at their work. So daring was the approach of these forerunners of the force, that the very audacity of their movements caused them to be mistaken for some of our own Soumali drivers, and it was a minute at least before they were detected and shot down.

This more than anything shows how completely
we were taken by surprise, and how utterly
ignorant we had been of any danger.

But I must refer back again to what became
of the Transport. By far the greater part were
killed and wounded at the first onslaught, but
when the stampede took place they very soon
scattered in all directions, and as far as the eye
could reach, all over the plain were camels,
riderless horses, mules kicking themselves free
of broken harness, drivers running for their
lives, and our own men cut off from the zaribas,
sharing a common fate with the rest, and falling
either speared by the enemy or shot down by
the reckless fire of some of the Native Infantry.
All those who were at first shut out from the
zaribas and swept away by the stampede of
animals were never able to reach the squares
again, as it was utterly impossible for them to
approach their friends when they had once
opened fire. Many attempted to do so, but
they had to turn before the storm and fly with
the rest in the direction of Suakin. Many of
the cavalry and a great part of the transport
men fled for their lives in this way ; some managed to leap on to the backs of affrighted
animals, and even these had to gallop hard

to escape from the numbers of Arabs who attempted to run them down, while others ran on foot, and few indeed of these ever reached the camp alive. Some escaped a fearful end by hiding in the bush and feigning death, and a lad of ours saved his life in this way by lying down between two comrades who had fallen down killed by the Arab bullets. They continued their pursuit to within a mile of the camp, and thus the whole line of retreat was covered with dead and general *débris*. The first and somewhat exaggerated account of the affair was conveyed to the camp by these refugees, many of whom reached home in time to tell the news in broken, breathless sentences, and then to fall and die.

The enemy's tactics were as well planned as they had been two days before, and they carried out an attack upon all sides simultaneously without any shouting or word of command, and without showing themselves for a moment. Not only this, but seeing our most vulnerable point was the transport, they got round in rear of the camels and other animals, and drove them before them on to the zaribas, thus not only being able to slaughter the transport at will, but also to drive them on to us and thus throw our own

men into confusion. A further force took up
a position on the path along which we had
advanced in the morning, ready to cut off our retreat to Suakin, and also to intercept all animals
which did not fall before the knives and spears
of the attacking party.

A very strong reserve, some thousands strong,
was also in readiness to carry out the massacre
at the zaribas, which they fully expected to
effect; and when they had completely exter-
minated our force here, it was their intention
to fall upon the camp before Suakin with their
whole force, after which the starving out of the
zariba at Hasheen would have been merely a
question of days. All this we found out afterwards from prisoners, but the disposition of
their forces showed us quite plainly enough
what their intentions were. They might, had
it not been for the gallantry of our troops, have
carried out the first part of their programme,
and it was a wonder they did not; but beyond
doing a certain amount of mischief among the
deserted part of the camp, they would have been
simply swept off the face of the earth by the
force left behind there, as there was in the camp
at the time the Brigade of Guards, the 53rd, a
greater part of the cavalry, and a battery of

Horse Artillery, to say nothing of a mountain battery of seven-pounder screw-guns, which were quite prepared to receive them, as well as sundry other details and detachments. There was, indeed, an alarm in the camp that the enemy were coming down, and every preparation was made to receive them ; but they never showed up, though large bodies of them were seen from the Hasheen zariba moving across in that direction.

The natives and people in the town of Suakin were in a tremendous state of excitement, and the most conflicting accounts were current there about the fate of the troops. Some of the refugees had galloped right into Suakin, where they told the most awful tales of the total extermination of the force, and of the death of the General and all his soldiers.

For an hour or more after the fighting was over, detached bodies of the enemy were to be seen pursuing single animals over the plain towards the sea. They killed most of these, though they took possession of some. Several of the camels and mules, many of which were wounded, made as if by instinct for Suakin, and a few actually succeeded in reaching the camp in an utterly exhausted condition, and covered with blood.

- The actual fighting was over in less than half an hour, but the enemy did not turn tail and run—not a bit of it. Many of them merely turned round and walked quietly away, while others withdrew sullenly, keeping up a fire upon us as they went.

The scene around, both inside and outside the zaribas, was one utterly indescribable. Little would be gained by trying to describe it, if indeed it were possible, by mere word-painting, to convey the dimmest notion of the appearance of the ground around us. The task would be a sickening one to the writer, for it would be to go over old sorrows and old hours of the most bitter anguish of heart. It were better to try and blot out what must always remain, I fear, too vividly in the minds of those who witnessed it ; and I, for one, care not to pander to the morbid love for horrors possessed by a few. God knows, there is sorrow, trouble, and afflic- tion enough in this wide, erring, sinful world without attempting to add to it unnecessarily, or rend the hearts of those of the opposite sex at home, who in their gentleness and refinement know little or nothing of war with all its attendant misery.

Let us draw a veil over this part of the picture,

and deal solely with that which tells of bravery, of loving acts of kindness—of cases where the man laid down the arm and nursed the sick and the wounded with the care and the tenderness of a woman. A battle-field may bring out all those qualities of brutality, of almost fiendish brutality, in a man, but it most assuredly brings out as well his noblest instincts. The acts, I say, of mercy, of self-sacrifice, of love, and complete devotion seen on a battle-field shine out as beacons in a night of roaring storm, and serve to guide men in after years who have before thought little, cared little, and considered others little, and whose lives were hardly what they might have been. I have seen men stand on such occasions with hot tears coursing each other down their cheeks while they gazed on the sufferings of some comrade. I have seen others give their all to the wounded when they were almost starving themselves; and I have known men ready to lay down their lives for a friend at once, cheerfully and without hesitation. Are these noble qualities? Then let all soldiers who have these opportunities when fighting for their country, and take advantage of them, be honoured in Old England as soldiers should be honoured, instead of being often treated with indifference,

and more often still kicked out into the streets
as "unfit for further service," when they have
risked their lives for the country which spurns
them when cripples, and finds no home for them
when they have lost health and strength in some
deadly climate. Our streets tell this tale too
often, and our country-side as well. An old
soldier is cared for where he has friends, but how
about when he has none?

For some hours the troops stood in position
lining the sides of the zaribas, momentarily expecting a renewal of the attack, as the Hasheen
force heliographed to the effect that a large
body of the enemy were marching in our direction, many of whom were mounted on camels.
Nobody was allowed to leave the ranks, except
those employed bringing in the wounded to the
doctors, who, as usual after a battle, had their
hands full. Our dead were all placed together
in rows inside the zariba, and those of the enemy
were carried outside ready for burial the next
morning.

Boxes of biscuits and tinned meat, water-tins,
trusses of compressed hay, and a multitude of
other things, were strewed about outside in all
directions, and as much of this as possible was
collected together, while the few remaining

camels and mules were also brought inside the
zaribas. Many of these luckless animals were
to be seen hobbling about wounded, or standing
up slowly bleeding to death. The inside of the
zariba seemed to be stained everywhere with
blood, and almost every one was spattered with
it. Many men, for the first few moments after
the fight was over, simply fell down from exhaustion and dropped off to sleep, so with their
blood-stained jackets it was difficult to tell who
was wounded and who was not. It was impossible to drag the dead bodies of the animals
outside the zaribas that night, as every one was
too tired to do anything but look after the
wounded. Of course the inside of the zariba
was littered with every imaginable thing—broken
rifles, spears, shields, swords, parts of kits, helmets,
empty cartridge-cases in thousands, blood-stained
caps and jackets, bayonets twisted in all sorts of
shapes, and thrown away as useless, and sundry
other things too numerous to mention.

Thus occurred in one short half-hour, and
suddenly in all the quiet of a Sunday afternoon,
one of the bloodiest fights ever chronicled.

Just when our people at home were sitting
in the stillness, perhaps, of some village church,
listening to the voice of a pastor offering up

the prayer to God, "from battle and murder, and from sudden death, good Lord, deliver us;" or, perchance, singing the words of some favourite hymn, or even, it may be, repeating the prayer for us soldiers; we were fighting and falling fast, while many a spirit was in one second wafted upward to appear before his Maker. It was as well they knew it not. On what to them must have been a peaceful sabbath morn—

> "That trysting-place of God and man; that link
> Betwixt a near eternity and time"—

was to us a scene of bloodshed and of death, of man fighting with man for very life, ay, and dashing out all semblance of the creature that God has set up here in His own image. To look on a scene such as we saw that day at those blood-stained zaribas is to be seized with a horror of war, and to say with the poet in all sincerity—

> "Avaunt thee, horrid War, whose miasms, bred
> Of nether darkness and Tartarean swamps,
> Float o'er this fallen world and blight the flowers,
> Sole relics of a ruin'd Eden ! Hence
> With all thy cruel ravages !—fair homes
> Rifled for thee of husband, brother, son ;
> Wild passions slipp'd like hell-hounds in the heart,
> And baying in full cry for blood ; the shock
> Of battle ; the quick throes of dying men ;
> The ghastly stillness of the mangled dead."

I remember the words of a great man who said, "While you are engaged in the field, many will repair to the closet, many to the sanctuary; the faithful of every name will employ that prayer which has power with God; the feeble hands which are unequal to any other weapon, will grasp the sword of the Spirit; and from myriads of humble, contrite hearts the voice of intercession, supplication, and weeping will mingle in its ascent to heaven with the shouts of battle and the shock of arms." And thus the force was delivered that day from a slaughter almost unparalleled in the annals of war, from a catastrophe which would have carried weeping and mourning into a thousand households, and made our country shake to her foundations, while people mute with horror looked each other in the face and realized, as one realizes the meaning of some faint far-off sound, what war really is.

The darkness at length closed around the zaribas and shut out from the eye for a time the ghastly sights around. There was perfect silence inside the three squares as a quarter of the force stood lining the hedges and peering into the night. No lights were to be seen except where the doctors worked incessantly at the mass of suffering around them. The dawn was breaking long before they had completed their sickening task. Many of the enemy had their wounds tied up with the same tenderness as if they had been our friends, and I think some of the most fearful wounds were those inflicted by the Snider bullets of the Indian troops. One had not, unfortunately, to look among the enemy only for these wounds, for many of our men will carry to their graves the results of the momentary panic.

While one quarter of the force guarded the front of the zaribas, the remainder slept on the blood-stained ground, ready at any moment to jump to their posts. There was one alarm that night due to a mule breaking away from the picketing lines, and being chased by one of the native drivers across the centre zariba. In a moment the whole of the men were in their places, firing away into the bush as fast as they could, so much had their nerves been shaken by the terrible events of the day. The "Cease fire!" was sounded, and immediately the former death-like stillness reigned around, broken now and then only by the neighing of a horse, or the grumble of a camel, or, what was worse, by the shrill and piteous cry of some wretched wounded

Arab, calling "Moya! Moya!" "Water! Water!"
as he lay in tortures in the bush. Then the
sound of a voice would come from afar off,
answering the wounded, as parties of the enemy
scoured the bush and carried off their friends.
Ever since dark the signalling party were
flashing an endless succession of messages to
the camp, and all night long this continued
without intermission. Lists of the killed and
wounded were in this way flashed in to head-
quarters, as well as many a message to friends
there, assuring of safety, and asking that the welcome news might be forwarded home to England.

It was not until after ten o'clock that the
moon rose and threw her white light over the
field. The scene looked, if possible, doubly
ghastly now, and one could see the dead lying
all round in hundreds, while numbers of the
enemy lay actually in heaps close up to the
zaribas.

The weary hours of the night dragged on
slowly, as we lay on the ground listening for
any sound and starting at the faintest noise.
At last the sky in the east began to show signs
of growing red, and never was dawn more welcome to men than it was to us that morning.
The night with all its anxiety was past, the

constant dread of an attack in the darkness
was over, and it mattered little what the day
brought, for we were ready now.

When the noise of the first heavy firing was
heard in the camp, and volumes of dust were
seen flying high in the air, there was a rush to
any point of vantage where a view could be
obtained of what was happening to the force
that had marched in the morning. It looked as
if a fearful catastrophe had happened; the fire
was very rapid and "independent," and there was
at first none of that regularity in it betokening
steadiness and obedience to commands. The
volumes of dust that filled the air showed that
either the cavalry were charging, or that large
bodies of the enemy were traversing the ground
with great rapidity. Then from out of the
volumes of dust and smoke appeared a mass of
fugitives, men and animals, and everywhere all
over the plain were to be seen riderless horses,
mules, and camels, flying for very life. At first
it appeared as though the whole force had been
scattered, but the rapid firing still continued, and
then after a while gradually settled down into
steady volleys. It was all right then; the men
were steady and in hand, and those volleys told
of security and of fearful slaughter.

There was immediate activity in the camp, and before the first fugitives arrived the whole of the force there were under arms. One battalion of Guards had started in the morning as escort to a convoy carrying out stores to the Hasheen zariba, but the other two battalions were at once paraded, and, together with a battery of Horse Artillery and a strong force of cavalry, marched in the direction of the zaribas. This force did not, however, go out more than about two miles, as the firing had entirely ceased. About six in the evening it was accordingly marched back again to camp, bringing with them in their dhoolies many wounded, who had sunk down in their flight from loss of blood and exhaustion.

Every preparation was made in the camp to repel an attack, and a greater part of the force was under arms and on the watch all night, while guns were got into position and tents were struck to clear the ground. It was a night of great anxiety for those in camp, owing to the uncertainty about what had actually happened. Many of those who had escaped gave conflicting accounts of the fight, while many friends were reported killed by them who turned up the following day all right. It was not, however,

O

till towards evening of the next day that a true
account of the affair reached the camp, and
anxiety was set at rest.

There are one or two things which need a
reference to do with this fight at the zaribas.
The first in importance is the clogging of the
Martini-Henry rifles. Years ago, when first
these rifles were issued to the army, every instructor of musketry was asked to send in a
report upon the way they worked in his regiment. The common fault found with them then
was that the extractor failed in the performance
of its proper functions, and that a rifle was often
rendered momentarily useless on account of the
inability to extract the cartridge-case after firing
without either repeatedly working the lever or
drawing the cleaning-rod and forcing the case
out by pressure from the muzzle. With regard
to the cartridge itself, fault was found with its
construction ; but we were informed that the
cartridge was only experimental, and would be
replaced by a better one later on. However
that may be, the clumsy built up and bottle-
shaped cartridge has been in use in the army
ever since, and no other cartridge has ever been
supplied ; and more than this, a price is given
per thousand for the empty cases returned into

store. Thus the cartridges are refilled and the error continued *ad infinitum.* As a musketry instructor, I used to dress all my markers with the money I obtained for the old cartridge-cases, and thus I was a party to the sin ; but I see no reason why all these built-up cartridges should not be got rid of at target practice, and reloaded as often as you like, provided they are not issued to men going on active service. It not unfrequently happened that the base of the cartridge was torn right off by the jaws of the extractor, when the rifle was at once rendered utterly useless. The sand and the temperature may have had a certain amount to do with the jamming, but the fault lay principally in the extractor of the rifle and the form of the cartridge. The extractor ought certainly to be improved upon if this rifle is to continue the arm of the services ; and a drawn copper cartridge-case, unlubricated, should take the place of the present one. Many men have lost their lives through these two things in our late wars ; and though years ago reports, as I say, were made by those best able to judge on the defects of the weapon and the cartridge, no notice was ever taken, and thus through a love of cheeseparing economy, and a penny wise and pound

foolish policy, valuable lives have been sacrificed.

Another thing to which I think attention
should be drawn is the bayonet. We hear a
lot about the wonderful quality of British steel;
but why are our soldiers armed with a weapon
which, when put to the test, simply doubles up
like so much soft metal? Surely, above all
others the weapons we give our soldiers to fight
with should be of the best possible quality. A
man going covert shooting is not contented to
go out armed with a thirty-shilling gun from
Birmingham, neither is a man going pig-sticking
content to have a soft piece of metal at the end
of his staff; but it seems perfectly natural to
those at home to send our soldiers out into the
field to fight their country's enemies with a rifle
which is liable to be rendered utterly useless at
any moment, and a bayonet as much use to
them as if it were made of hoop-iron. Every
soldier's life is valuable, and our soldiers are not
so numerous that we can afford to sacrifice them
to the love of economy of some, and the short-
sighted policy and indifference of some few
more. A jammed rifle may be of use to the
man who can go in with the bayonet, but how
about a rifle with a bent bayonet in front of the

muzzle? The first is bad enough, but in the
latter case the weapon is rendered utterly useless. In every fight in the Sûdan campaign
there were many instances of both of these
faults, and surely it is time, therefore, some
notice was taken of a crying evil which may
land us in a terrible plight when we become
engaged in a European war. Our swords want
looking to as well; the present pattern cavalry
sword is made of bad metal, the job of some
contractor. All bayonets and swords should be
called in and a fresh issue made of weapons,
each of which have been put through a severe
test similar to that through which Mr. Wilkinson
puts his celebrated blades, to the satisfaction
of the purchaser.

The Gardner guns always appeared to jam,
but of course, in a complicated weapon of this
kind, the conditions under which it was tried
in the Sûdan were a severe test. The expansion
of the metal from the heat, and the dust which
was always flying about, were sufficient in a
great measure to account for its failure; but I
think the cartridge was also at fault here. Later
on in the campaign another form of Gardner
gun came out, consisting of two barrels, enclosed
in a cylinder filled with a fluid, instead of the five

exposed barrels as in the ordinary pattern gun.
I am not aware that this gun ever came into action,
but it was tried at Suakin with good results.

The ammunition was of two kinds in the
Suakin force—a fatal error. Why cannot the
Indian troops be armed with the Martini instead
of the Snider? One word about the revolver.
The calibre of the regulation pattern revolver a
short time ago was ·450, but it has lately been
changed to ·455, so that there were again two
different sizes of ammunition here. Moreover,
the ammunition was of an inferior quality, and I
heard on one occasion of three miss fires out of
six—a nice thing to happen when everything may
depend upon a shot! The calibre of the revolvers should be increased ; the present bullet is
not sufficient to stop a man unless he is struck
in the head or the heart, and an Arab shield
made of crocodile skin or rhinoceros hide would,
we found, turn a revolver bullet at forty yards.
A revolver is ten times more use than a sword,
provided it is fitted with the Webley patent,
enabling the user to reload without difficulty.
All cavalrymen, gunners, and sergeants of infantry should be armed with them, and prizes
offered for good shooting, as practice with the
weapon should be encouraged. A revolver is a

most difficult weapon to use with effect, and it is useless in the hands of a novice.

Before closing this chapter, the losses in the zariba fight have to be chronicled. As to the loss sustained by the enemy, they must have had, at the lowest possible computation, twelve hundred killed. We collected and buried a thousand and more of these poor fellows, nearly all of whom were the Mahdi's men and not the common Hadendowa tribesmen, as they wore the white blouse and straw cap which makes up the uniform of the Prophet's soldiers. For every man killed there must have been at least one wounded, so two thousand four hundred killed and wounded would be within the mark.

As to our own losses, they were very heavy, and especially so in transport animals. The official account which I obtained from a friend, better than all others able to judge, was as follows :—

Seven officers killed and five wounded. Sixty-six rank and file killed and one hundred and twenty wounded, and one officer and one hundred and twenty-four men missing. Besides this, we had in the water column alone one hundred and seventy-nine native drivers killed and missing out of a total of considerably under three hundred who started in the morning ; and it would not be too much to say that there were fifty more drivers killed in the Commissariat convoy. As to the loss sustained in animals, I am unable to give any figures regarding either mules or horses, but our loss in camels was six hundred and eighty-two ; our gross loss on this and the succeeding day being eight hundred and twenty camels. The value of these animals may be estimated as follows : The Egyptian camels for the most part were bought at prices averaging £20 apiece, and they then had to be brought to Suez and shipped to Suakin, so that when delivered at the Camel Depôt, Suakin, their cost to the country must have been £25 per head. The Indian and Berbera camels were bought at a lower figure, but taking into consideration the distance they had to be brought, they must have averaged at least £20 per head. It will never be known how many of each class there were out that day, but our water transport was mainly composed of Indian camels, and we lost over four hundred of them ; so, taking two-thirds of the animals killed at £20 apiece and the remaining one-third at £25 apiece, the nett loss to the country in camels would stand at £17,765. This, it must be remembered, is exclusive of horses and mules, and there were a great number of these killed besides.

It remains a fact that cannot be contradicted or gainsaid, that this terrible loss of life was occasioned by neglect in taking proper precautions, and a foolhardy carelessness combined with a total disregard of the most ordinary military principles. The force was halted in the wrong place to begin with, and had the line of country more towards the sea been adopted, the enemy, if they had attacked us at all, would have done so at great disadvantage, as there is there much less bush, and we should have been apprised of their approach. We should have been also in an equally good position as a halting-place on the road to Tamai, and more protected from any attacks while the depôt was forming. Instead of this, we were marched into a thick impenetrable jungle, thereby giving all the advantage to the enemy and putting a surprise at a premium. Sufficient precautions were not taken to protect the force while working at the zaribas—why, nobody knows. The result was what? A surprise.

It is easy to appear wise after the event, but I am merely writing here what occurred to the minds of all of us actually at the time.

I was told afterwards that our Intelligence Department out there had received news through their spies that it was the intention of the enemy to attack us that day, and that they would watch their opportunity. From the source I heard this, I believe it to be the truth.

I have no wish to be critical. I confine myself to facts in telling this story, and I leave others to comment and to make further inquiries. There were grave mistakes committed that day, but why those mistakes were committed there are others better able to judge than I am. It is their duty to inquire.

CHAPTER IX.

CONVOYS.

ALMOST before day had broken every one was astir in the zaribas, and parties were sent out at once to search the bush for any of our dead and wounded. Two or three of the enemy's banners were picked up, and any rifles collected and brought in. Most of the banners taken had inscriptions on them ; some were white with red edges, others blue, and one was black. The enemy were seen hovering about the zaribas, and two or three times in the morning they opened fire, when the men were immediately ordered to stand to their arms. Under these circumstances it was difficult to get on with any work. Large holes were being dug in the sand to bury the dead in, as this, for sanitary reasons, had to be attended to at once, and the air was already filled with a sickly smell.

Our killed were buried with the greatest

decency circumstances would permit, and the officers were interred in two separate graves. We had, of course, to bury the Arabs as best we could ; huge holes were made and as many placed in them as possible, the sand being afterwards heaped high over the grave. It was impossible to do anything with the enormous number of dead animals ; those nearest to the zaribas were dragged away, and some were covered in ; but our only hope was the birds, who very soon congregated in great numbers. Many wounded Arabs still lay about near the zariba ; it was dangerous work, though, walking near them, as they invariably endeavoured to reach passers-by with any weapon they still possessed. A young officer was killed by one of these wounded Arabs shortly after the fight ; he went outside the zariba, and as he passed by the hedge forming the side of the defence, a wounded Arab raised himself from the ground and ran him through the back with his spear. The officer turned round and re-entered the zariba, but he was unable to speak, and fell down dead almost directly afterwards. One of our men, too, taking pity on a wounded Arab, gave him his water-bottle. The Arab took the bottle and drained it, and when he handed it back he accompanied it with a thrust from a knife, which dangerously wounded the man, in return for his kindness. There were other instances of this kind, but I mention the two cases above in order to show how deep-seated was the hatred of the Arabs for us, and how perfectly ready they were to die, happy if they could first only get an opportunity of dyeing their spears in the blood of an infidel. It is not to be wondered at that our men, after experiences of this sort, killed the wounded as they lay on the ground, and it is unfortunately only too true that this occurred on several occasions. I have no wish to plead in their defence, however much provocation they may have had ; on the contrary, I think this course was unnecessary ; and though war must always have, to a certain extent, a brutalizing effect upon men, I do not see why members of a civilized race should pay off barbarians in their own coin. To do so is to descend to their level, and to be as much barbarians as they are. The Arabs endeavoured to take advantage of us when they were wounded because they were impelled by a wild fanaticism, and there is no doubt also that they mutilated our dead ; but this is no reason why we should do the same, unless it were in indi-

vidual cases of self-defence.   We should shrink
with horror from mutilating a dead body, but
to kill a wounded man is worse.   The Arabs
knew no better, but we did.   Kindness they did
not understand, and gratitude was foreign to
them ; the first they looked upon as weakness,
the second as an impossibility from a Mohammedan to a Christian.   The only extenuating
circumstance I can find to do with this killing
the wounded is, that our men were for the time
demoralized by the fierceness of the fighting,
and lost control of themselves ; and I believe
many were embittered by seeing friends fall
after the fighting was over.   However this may
be, the practice was not continued, and was of
course immediately discouraged and forbidden
by the officers.   I do not wish the reader to
imagine that our men went out into the bush
and killed the wounded off indiscriminately ;
this was not the case.   Many wounded Arabs,
on the contrary, had their wounds dressed by
our doctors, and were given food and water,
being afterwards carried out into the bush again
to be fetched away by their own people.   Many
of the Arab wounded entreated our people to
kill them, in order that they might be despatched
to a happy land by the hand of the infidel.

At about twelve o'clock in the day (23rd of March) a strong force arrived at the zariba from the camp, consisting of the brigade of Guards, some cavalry, and mounted infantry, enclosing a large convoy of water and stores. This force was not attacked during their march out along the line of flight the night before. All along the road there were lying dead men, horses, and camels ; but no halt was made to bury any of these, as the General wished to reach the zaribas as soon as possible.

After an hour or two for rest it was arranged that the Grenadiers, together with the whole of the Indian Infantry, should accompany the convoy back to camp ; the Scots and Coldstreams being left behind in the centre zariba. Preparations were shortly after made for the return, and a huge square formed, the Grenadiers bringing up the rear. All the wounded that it was possible to send in were sent with this square, a large number of dhoolies and dhoolie-bearers having been brought out.

Shortly after three o'clock we turned our backs on the blood-stained zaribas and commenced our march home.

And now began a hurried and most ill-managed affair. There were a vast number of

camels to be taken back to camp ; as, besides
all those we had brought with us in the morning,
there were also the whole of the animals collected in the zaribas after the fighting was over ;
and together with these there were many mule-
carts, ambulances, and our long train of wounded.

About two miles after leaving the zaribas our
leaders began to think that, hampered as we
were with this vast collection of animals, we
should not reach the camp before darkness set in
unless means were taken to increase the pace.
Orders were accordingly given to press forward as
quickly as possible, and a general thrashing of the
wretched transport animals began ; not, however,
carried out by the Transport themselves, but by
those inexperienced in the management of
camels, and ignorant of the pace a camel can
travel.   In this way loads were dropped and not
picked up, saddles were torn off and lost, as no
halt was made to reorganize the convoy, and
speed was attained at the sacrifice of everything
else.   What was the result ?   Our march, instead
of resembling the return of a victorious army,
resembled only a disorganized rabble retiring as
rapidly as they could before a pursuing foe.
Confusion was everywhere, order there was
none ; and the camp was reached at last just

before sunset in a state of disorganization. In
our wake were empty boxes, parts of saddlery,
exhausted camels, and in fact the ground might
have conveyed to the Arabs the appearance of
a general rout. "Get on, get on," said our
superiors; and we did "get on," but at what
sacrifice? Had it not been for the Grenadiers
who, as I said just now, brought up the rear in
line, the confusion would have been ten times
worse. The Sikhs did good service as well;
but the whole thing was a disgrace to any
civilized army, and reflected only renewed mis-
management on the part of those responsible.
I have endeavoured to give a mild impression of
this return of ours to camp, but there are many
who might paint it in far more glaring colours.
I confine my remarks to the simple impressions
of an eye-witness.

That night we were hard at work loading up
water again for the convoy, starting the following morning at daybreak, as we very often at
this time worked all night long, and then
marched and fought all day. It was hard work,
very hard work in that climate, where it was
always intensely hot, where there was never a
cloud in the sky, and where food and water
were scarce. The heat had become very much

P

greater since our arrival, and every day the sun seemed to be growing in strength. Sickness was much on the increase, and men were dropping fast from sunstroke, exhaustion, and fever ; for the never-ending fatigues, escorts, and " sentry go " was telling on the men very much.

It was the intention of the General to collect a great quantity of stores of all kinds at the zaribas preparatory for the further advance to Tamai, consequently every day all through this week convoys of provisions and enormous quantities of water were sent out there. This convoy work was very heavy on all concerned, as the march was a long one, being over five miles out and five miles home, over burning sand and through thick and thorny bush. Moreover, the convoys were almost always attacked going out or coming home, and not unfrequently both ways, so little were the enemy overcome by their two very recent defeats.

The escort this particular morning was composed of the 15th Sikhs and 28th Bombay Native Infantry, with a party of Madras Sappers, and a body of cavalry consisting of a squadron of the 9th Bengal, and another of the 20th Hussars. The orders were that they were to march out three miles, and commence to cut a

" drift " and form a zariba. A force was to be
sent out from the zariba to meet them and take
over the convoy.

The home force was not interfered with on
their march out, reaching the point where they
were to construct their zariba without seeing
anything of the enemy.

About eleven o'clock a battalion of the Guards
(Coldstreams) and the Marines, left the zaribas
to meet the convoy half-way, and were almost
immediately fired upon by large parties of the
enemy who were seen to be swarming in the
surrounding bush. Most of the bullets flew
high over the square, but one officer and one
man of the Marines were wounded.

The two parties met at about two o'clock, and
the two wounded were given over to the Indian
Infantry, who then recommenced their march
home.

The Guards and Marines, accompanied by
the cavalry, were twice attacked on their way
back to the zaribas. Not long after leaving the
Indian regiments, large bodies of the enemy
suddenly dashed from the bush and charged
down on our force with the utmost impetuosity.
The cavalry clearing the front, enabled the
Guards and Marines to open fire, which they

did with the utmost effect, the enemy after a
while retiring into the bush again and out of
sight. For some while it was supposed that
another heavy attack similar to that of Sunday
was intended, as great numbers of the enemy
were seen both from the squares as well as from
the zaribas ; but after the first rush, when many
of the Arabs got close up to our bayonets and
engaged our men hand-to-hand, they did not
for a time attempt to renew the attack, con-
tenting themselves with firing long shots at us
from the bush. The enemy having retired, the
force again moved forward, but was a second time
attacked shortly before reaching the zaribas,
though not by large numbers. The losses
sustained by the enemy must have been, from
all accounts and from the bodies we saw lying
about on the following day, upwards of two
hundred killed ; while we on our side had three
killed and thirteen wounded.

From the zaribas considerable bodies of the
enemy were seen drawn up on the right while
this attack on the convoy was being carried on,
and their strength was variously estimated as
from four to six thousand men. Endeavours
were made to reach them with the Gardner
guns, but they were just out of range. Had

there only been a part of the mountain battery in the zaribas, they could have plied them with their shells with the most deadly effect, and destroyed numbers before they could have with-drawn into a position of safety.

The bravery displayed by the enemy on this occasion was as marked as on all others. They simply appeared perfectly callous of the punish-ment they received, and their heavy losses of only two days before did not seem to have affected them in the least. As to our having established a funk among them, that was pure nonsense. Their valour was as marked as it was before, and they were only embittered by the chastise-ment they had undergone. Women and boys were again seen in their ranks supplying the fighting men with arms and ammunition, and altogether the number of men who appeared ready to fight for the cause of the Mahdi seemed to be absolutely unlimited. It certainly looked as though there were plenty always prepared to charge our squares, or to throw themselves on to our bayonets, in spite of the example made of those who had come before.

The following morning another convoy was despatched to the zaribas, carrying a large supply of water.

It was on this occasion that our balloon was
first used, and it was also memorable as being
the first occasion on which we had ever made
use of a balloon on active service.   The balloon,
which was of goldbeater's skin, covered with a
netting, was taken up to the Right Water Fort
the night before and unpacked in the ditch,
when filling it was at once commenced, so that
it should be ready to ascend by daybreak next
morning.

When I reached the Water Fort just before
daylight, after a hard night's work loading up
water, I found the balloon inflated and quite
ready for the ascent.   I was rather disappointed
at its size, and fully expected to see a larger one.
The basket or carriage beneath the balloon did
not seem capable of holding more than one
person.   The actual measurement of the balloon
was twenty-three feet in diameter, and its weight
altogether ninety pounds.   When filled it contained seven thousand cubic feet of gas, brought
all the way from Chatham, a distance of nearly
four thousand miles.

Very soon after our convoy was formed up
ready to start, the balloon began to rise slowly
to a height of about two hundred feet, being
fastened to the ground by two lines attached to

the car. An admiring crowd of natives witnessed the ascent in silence, and did not seem
in the least surprised, much to my disappointment, as I had expected to see them struck
with amazement at the sight of a man floating
about in the air. However, these natives seem
astonished at nothing, and I do not believe they
would have been surprised if they had seen a
regiment provided with wings and suddenly begin
to fly. Whether the extreme unexcitability of
temperament of these people is the result of
dulness of intellect, or that they are altogether
emotionless, I do not know, but they were not
taken by surprise at the sight of the balloon,
looking on the whole while with far less interest
than is shown by an average London crowd wit-
nessing the departure of a party of gentlemen in
a balloon from the lawns of the Crystal Palace. I
fear that the excellent stories concocted for the
delectation of the people at home about the Arabs
being struck dumb with horror at the sight of
the balloon, or flying in masses and hiding themselves from the sight of this terrible apparition,
are nothing more or less than humbug. The
behaviour of the " friendlies " may be taken as
being that of the Arabs, who were neither dis-
mayed nor deterred from any action they may

have determined on by the sight of the balloon
flying in the air above them.   When the convoy
was ready to move, the balloon, still two hundred feet up, was made fast to a cart in the
centre of the square.   It was rather difficult to
avoid jerking the cords which held it, and thus
running the chance of breaking them ; but extreme care was taken when crossing any rough
pieces of ground, as it would not have been
pleasant for the occupant of the car if he had
suddenly found himself floating quietly towards
the mountains miles beyond the reach of any
friends.

Communication was kept up with the balloon
by means of written messages, and it was not
long before a letter came down telling us that
the enemy were still pursuing the stampeded
camels down towards the sea and killing them
as soon as they got up with them.   The enemy
could also be seen in force retiring in the Tamai
direction ; and later on a large body of them
were standing gaping up at the balloon only
three or four hundred yards distant from the
convoy, though quite unseen by us on the
ground.

The force reached the zaribas at last un-
molested, when the balloon was hauled down

and packed up, the gas being as far as possible saved for future use. Thus the first ascent may be chronicled as a success.

The convoy returned to Suakin in the evening without firing a shot.

The stench all around the zaribas was simply terrible. It was absolutely impossible to bury the dead camels lying in hundreds in the bush, and there are few things that stink more fearfully than a dead camel. I have known them to scent the air strongly when their bodies have been at least a mile off. Added to the camels, many of the enemy's dead remained unburied about the country; our friends, the birds, too, were surfeited with their loathsome meal, and hopped about lazily or stood unable to move or get out of one's way, being simply gorged to repletion.

Life in the zariba was almost unendurable. As much shelter as possible was obtained by sticking blankets or waterproof sheets on to spears, thus making a sort of awning. Any shade that could be got behind the cases of stores or the forage-bags was seized upon at once, as the heat all day was terrific.

Water was sparingly issued, and at one time the ration was reduced as low as one pint per

man in the morning and another pint in the
evening. This, to wash in, cook in, and live on,
was little enough when all the food that could
be got was bouilli beef and hard biscuit, which
last it was impossible to eat without first soak-
ing. Why the ration of water was reduced so
low I know not, as there were upwards of forty
thousand gallons stored in the zaribas in large
tanks buried in the sand. I remember hearing
at this time of a bottle of soda-water fetching
half a sovereign ; the purchaser did not, however, proceed to drink it at once, but, slowly and
solemnly pulling out the cork, he washed his
face in it. And here I want to correct a wrong
impression which we saw afterwards was much
commented on in the papers sent out to us from
home. It was reported in one that the supply
of water was accumulating very slowly at the
zaribas, and the troops there were on short
allowance, as through some bungling empty tins
and barrels had been sent out in one convoy.
To this it is only necessary to give a most
emphatic denial ; it was absolutely impossible
that it could have happened. Every tin was
locked, after being filled, by a responsible person,
who was more often than not an officer ; special
parties being told off by us to look after this

important point. The filled tins were afterwards placed in rows along the railway, another officer seeing them put in the trucks previous to their being taken on to the camel lines ; and an empty tin could not have escaped him. Every tin and barrel was shortly after placed in the *celitas* and packed on the camels. I am therefore absolutely certain no tin or barrel ever started in our convoys empty. Some of the barrels leaked very much, and there may have been robbery ; but the other assertion is absurd, and it probably was a story started by some person who got mixed up in his hot haste for information between the outgoing convoy with full tins and the returning convoy with the empty ones. Thus, in his excessive zeal to discover a mare's nest, he may have tumbled against an empty load, and started a false report detrimental to a department who worked harder than any other all through the war, and never failed.

The condensed water was good enough when it was fresh, but after being kept a day or so in the tins it began to smell and became filled with a white slime. I never heard how this slime was accounted for. Certainly condensed water will always extract its salts from other bodies if possible, and the material of which the tanks

were made, galvanized iron, or the solder, may
have had something to do with it; but however
this was, the water was not wholesome, and I
cannot help thinking that some means might
have been adopted by which it might have
been in a measure aërated. Sickness was increasing very rapidly at this time in the zaribas,
there being several cases of enteric fever. The
disease most prevalent was dysentery. I put
this down almost entirely to the want of fresh
meat, which might so easily have been sent out
from Suakin. The bouilli beef which, as I mentioned before, was rather salt, was principally
the cause of it, and why the army was ever
supplied with such uneatable and unsuitable
stuff is wonderful indeed. I knew many cases
where men actually threw their rations away
rather than run the chance of increasing their
thirst by putting such stuff in their mouths.
A few potatoes were issued, but why was there
not a plentiful supply of lime-juice served out
daily? It would have been as simple a thing
as possible to have allowed the troops at the
zaribas a ration of fresh meat at least twice
a week. A few oxen or sheep might have been
driven out with the convoys and slaughtered on
arrival at the zaribas, if it had been considered

unadvisable to send dead meat out in carts.
This last method might, too, have been easily
managed, as a plentiful supply of ice was always
procurable from the ships. Instead of this, the
men were fed on an eternal supply of tinned
meats, till every one was simply nauseated with
the stuff and turned from it with loathing and
disgust. An eminent medical man out there
told me that dysentery might have been almost
entirely avoided had fresh meat been sent out
twice a week, and that, from certain symptoms
he observed, he discovered that the force in the
zaribas was bordering on scurvy. A nice thing
to happen when there was a plentiful supply of
fresh meat only six miles off!

The sick were always sent in by the returning
convoys, and every care taken of them while at
the zaribas, the doctors being simply inde-
fatigable.

A telegraph wire had been laid along the
ground when we advanced on Sunday, but this
was always being cut by the natives, who had
a wholesome horror of wires after their experiences of the mines laid round Suakin. This
difficulty was overcome by building a crow's
nest at the zaribas, which served the double
purpose of a signalling station and a look-out

post. All messages were sent in to the Right
Water Fort, from which point they were forwarded on to the different parts of the camp.
The signalling party at the zaribas were very
hardly worked, and were often up till late at
night, when the lamps took the place of the
heliograph. Of course it soon became apparent
to the Arab mind that the force in the zaribas
was dependent for supplies on the camp, and no
doubt their having grasped this was the cause
of the perpetual attacks on the convoys. We
heard through our spies that Osman Digna had
given orders to the effect that the zaribas were
not to be attacked, but that everything was to
be done to harass the convoys, and all energy
was to be directed towards intercepting them
if possible. Hence they scarcely ever left us
alone.

The convoy escort duty fell doubly heavily on
the troops at this time, as, besides the labour
entailed on throwing provisions and water daily
into the zaribas, and thus collecting sufficient
supplies for the advance on Tamai, the Hasheen
zariba had also to be kept going in food and
water. So convoys were running in both directions. On Wednesday, the 25th of March, it was
therefore determined to withdraw the force from

the Hasheen zariba altogether, and that evening
the 70th and other details returned to camp,
escorted by a party of Mounted Infantry. During
their retreat the enemy were sighted and a few
shells fired into them, but beyond this the march
was uninterrupted.

The zariba was destroyed before leaving it,
and nothing then remained of our fight at
Hasheen beyond the graves down at the harbour of the poor fellows who had fallen in that
most objectless action. I say "objectless"
because few of us ever understood why lives
were sacrificed for so small an end.

We did not take the wells at Hasheen, and
thus interfere with the enemy's water supply.
The position at Hasheen did not protect the
right flank of the force advancing on Tamai, or
the line of communications either in the Handoub direction or the Tamai direction, for it was
many miles away from both. As to the protection it afforded to the flank of the force at the
zaribas, it was pretty evident on Sunday, the
22nd of March, that the Hasheen force was im-
potent to act in this direction. How far an
isolated force of one battalion was intended to
protect the line of communications may be
judged of by the fact that it was withdrawn

before the advance on Tamai began, and as soon as it had been determined that the army was to strike for Es Sibil. The force left at the Hasheen zariba was an isolated force, a weak force, and a useless force in the position it was placed. It absorbed a number of men who were much wanted elsewhere, and increased the amount of convoy duty when every one in the whole army was overworked as it was.

So the Hasheen zariba was destroyed, and the battle of Hasheen rendered as barren in results as it had been objectless in aim. The many acts of bravery performed on that day, and the gallant conduct of our troops, will always remain a monument to the British soldier, while the battle will only be recalled to mind by the graves of those who sleep beneath the sand.

The usual convoy was despatched at daybreak the next morning, and we rather expected to have a fight because we had been allowed to go in peace the day before. Our convoy was a large one and our escort strong, and as by this time we had cut a fairly open road all the way out to the zaribas, we were quite ready to give the Arabs a warm reception if they came on.

Sure enough, after getting about four miles out a heavy fire was opened on us from the bush, and several of our men were struck, but the greater part of the bullets flew over our heads.

About four thousand of the enemy then attacked us furiously on all sides with their usual astounding bravery. Many of them jogged in their peculiar manner right up to the square before they fell, while others walked quietly back again into the bush after endeavouring to penetrate our ranks. Their coolness under fire was simply astonishing, they seemed to care nothing about it ; and it was marvellous indeed that day after day men could be found to charge three or four battalions of infantry in the face of the awful slaughter that invariably took place.

Scores and scores of them fell on this occasion as on others, and remained there unburied to taint the air with sickening odours.

Once or twice on our return march from the zaribas we found the enemy had scraped together a thin covering of sand over the bodies of those slain in the morning, and these were very often unavoidably uncovered again as we traversed the path home.

Out at the zaribas•the stench was something frightful. The wind had blown away the sand, and thus partially uncovered the heaps of slain,

Q

leaving swollen and distorted limbs to fester in
the sun.

Added to other diseases contracted at the
zaribas, many suffered terribly with their eyes,
from the poisonous dust and the perpetual white
glare of the sand. I knew men who were completely blinded in this way, and who did not
recover their sight until many weeks afterwards.
Ophthalmia and similar diseases were prevalent,
and there were, of course, many cases of sunstroke. I think the greatest number on one day
occurred in one of our convoys, when we had
thirty men knocked over by the sun alone. I
saw cases where men dropped down suddenly,
as if they had been struck a heavy blow on the
head.

The day of the general advance was, of course,
kept a profound secret, and we only inferred it
must be before long from different little incidents
around us. The masses of stores that had now
been collected at the zaribas, the bringing in the
Hasheen force, the striking of the greater part of
the camp, as well as the numberless reports that
were flying about, all pointed to the fact that a
big fight would come off very soon. One thing
only was considered likely to defer the advance
for a while, and that was that our Australian

brothers had not arrived as yet, though they were expected almost daily. We all thought that if the enemy would only meet us at Tamai in force, we should then have an opportunity of fighting a decisive action, and crippling Osman to such an extent that he would be unable to carry on the war any longer. If this was likely to be the case, it seemed hard that we should start before the Australians arrived, and there was an earnest desire on the part of the whole army that they might come in time to share any fighting with us, and thus have an opportunity of showing the material of which they were made. We all looked forward to their arrival tremendously, and were prepared to give them a fitting welcome on landing.

We were very busy all Thursday night preparing for Friday's convoy, but very early in the morning orders came down saying that there would be nothing sent out to the zaribas, and that the troops would be employed striking their camps and sending spare baggage in to the caravanserai at Suakin. Friday came, therefore, as a welcome day of rest after a week of marching, of fighting, and incessant toil. The truth was that every one was overdone; the perpetual marching backwards and forwards to the zaribas

during the day, in a sun heat of over 160°, the large
number of men required every night for picket
duty, and the numbers also on night fatigues of
various kinds, was rapidly undermining the
strength and nerves of the men, and rendering
the whole force unfit for work. It was, therefore, wisely determined to give us all a day off;
but I do not mean by this that we had a complete holiday, for there was quite enough to be
done to make up an average day's hard work
without marching a convoy.

We were very busy packing up a few things
we wanted with us, such as a second flannel
shirt and another pair of socks, and so on; but
the largest part of our baggage was made up
of a

> " simple box of deal,
> Directed to no matter where ;
> And on it was this mute appeal,
> With Care ! "

There was something else we painted on this
box of deal, though, just by way of satisfying
any over-inquisitive minds, and at the same time
putting to rest the suspicions of the hungry, and
that was " Military Documents."

It was a great feat that, and the cause of
much merriment, as we quietly emptied everything out of the box, and put in with the greatest

care a bottle or two of whisky, several tins of Brand's essence of meat, cocoa and milk, potted meats, and sardines. With this store we thought four of us would be able to hold out as far as Tamai and back, and have some to give to hungry friends besides.

There were the wildest possible rumours going the round of the camp to explain why the advance was put off. The first was that the Mahdi had been made a prisoner by King John of Abyssinia, and that Osman had therefore decided to give himself up, and was expected in camp either to-night or to-morrow morning. To back this up, a flag of truce was said to have been seen flying in front of the camp; but this afterwards proved to be an old deal biscuit box distorted in the mirage. The Government, we were told, had decided to give up the war, and had telegraphed out to stop the railway at once. Of course, there were all sorts of stories about war with Russia and our future destination; how some regiments were to be sent on to India, and how the rest of the force was to be conveyed at once to Cyprus ready to operate in Asia Minor. One hour war had been actually declared, another that it had not, and so on. But these reports caused a deal of amusement, and gave us some-

thing to talk about; and though few of us
believed a word we heard, we used to discuss
the news with the utmost gravity.

Saturday's convoy reached the zaribas without
any particular incident, beyond being fired upon
by the enemy at a distance, and the return
was equally peaceable. · Each convoy always
brought back a number of sick, who were
generally taken down to the base hospital at
" H " Redoubt, and transferred to the *Ganges*,
or *Bulimba*, on the following day.

If we who had been living for the most part
in camp longed for the advance on Tamai, it may
be judged how much more eager the force in the
zaribas were to get out of their pestilential surroundings. The Scots Guards had been replaced by the Grenadiers, but the rest of the
force remained the same as at first. There was
nothing to be done to break the monotony of the
life there. There was, of course, occupation,
and the zaribas could always be improved and
strengthened, but excitement there was none ;
the enemy never ventured to attack them, and
on two or three occasions only did they fire a
few shots. Beyond this the day was only relieved by the meal of eternal "soup," and the issue
of water, or the watching for the approaching

convoy. There were a few newspapers of a certain antiquity to be read, and the rest of the day
was made up in trying to make work to employ
time. It was, of course, impossible to go any
distance away from the zaribas, as the enemy
were always on the watch to cut off any who
showed themselves.

In camp we had for the most part struck all
our tents and were bivouacking at night on the
ground. I was very much struck with the heavy
dews at night-time, and once or twice in the
morning the coat in which I had wrapped myself before going to sleep was quite wet through.
The dew did not show on the sand at all,
probably because it absorbed it at once, but it
soaked through a blanket or coat. The only
way to account for it was, I suppose, that the
intense heat exhaled by the sand met the colder
air coming in from the sea in the early morning,
and thus condensation took place. We never
felt any ill effects from it as it dried very quickly.
There were a good many cases of severe rheu-
matism, but this was most probably due to the
extreme variation in temperature between the
sun heat of the day and the cooler air of the
early dawn, when the thermometer sometimes
fell as low as 60°.

We never had any renewal of the night attacks on the camp, though a party were on one occasion detected crawling towards the Ordnance store. Precautions were not lessened, and strong pickets and double sentries were mounted as usual; so at length we lay down on the ground at night with the most comfortable pillow, a saddle, under our heads, and slept till morning with an easy conscience, but very often somewhat empty insides.

CHAPTER X.

TAMAI.

" BRAVO Australia!" I think this was what
we all felt as we saw the Colonial contingent
arrive in camp on Sunday, the 29th of March. We
gave them a regular hearty reception, and they
were cheered all along their road out, while the
bands of the various regiments in camp headed
the column playing many a tune familiar to all
Englishmen and Australians alike. The contingent were a fine-looking lot of fellows, and
appeared as if they were as fit as possible for
work. They all wore the familiar red serge coat,
albeit rather strange out here, but they very
soon changed into kharkee like the rest of us.
Every one from the highest to the lowest was
anxious to get a glimpse of them, and their
arrival quite brightened us all up, as we were at
that time rather depressed by our general surroundings. In after years, no doubt, this event

will be a landmark to look back to. Let us hope
the readiness with which our Australian and
Canadian colonies came forward voluntarily,
and extended to the mother country the hand of
help, when surrounded with a sea of troubles
unparalleled in her history, may serve as a
warning to our foes of the latent strength of the
British Empire, and at the same time be the beginning of that great Imperial Federation which
is to bind the whole together in one indissoluble
union for the protection of our commerce, the
defence of our possessions, and the supremacy of
our Country's flag.

The contingent were inspected by the General
on arrival in camp, and I am sure he echoed the
thoughts of all of us when he said, " In the name
of the force I command I give you a hearty
welcome. You are our comrades-in-arms, who
will share the perils, toils, and, I hope, glories of
this expedition. We honour the feeling which
led you to leave your pleasant homes to war
against the desert and its savage inhabitants.
You are soldiers as well as Englishmen. The
eyes of our common country are on you, and I
am sure you will do credit to the splendid
colony which sent you out, and the race to
which you belong." Cheer after cheer rent the

air after this, and we hoped the contingent were
as pleased with their reception as we were to
have them in our midst.

They were very proud of themselves, and
evidently delighted at forming part of such a
splendid force as we were in the Sûdan. I
shall never forget a man, fully six feet six
inches high, with a back as broad and as flat as
a billiard-table, and with a long black beard on
his face, coming up to me and saying, with the
utmost pride in his manner, "I am a representative of the New South Wales contingent ; can
you direct me to the camp?" The way he
drew himself up when he said, "I am a representative," showed at once that he thought the
New South Wales contingent ranked first, and
the rest nowhere. A spirit like this is worth a
regiment of soldiers ; and, though I wish to be
no croaker, I fear there is too much cause to say
that the day when every English soldier thought
there was only one regiment in the service and
only one company in that regiment—his own—
is fast passing away. And why ? Because of
the never-ending meddlesome interference which
can and will leave nothing alone, which strikes
at *esprit de corps* and destroys it root and branch,
which sacrifices everything to the recommenda-

tions of ignorant theorists, who bow down and worship the image of a false economy, and fawn to the powers that be.

The next two days were days of great weariness, as nothing is so trying to soldiers as inaction. Plenty of occupation and hard work is the surest way to maintain the health and spirits, and therefore the efficiency, of an army in the field.

I do not know why the advance was delayed. We were quite ready, and there were plenty of supplies of all sorts at the zariba, and water enough for the whole force for two days and more. Still we delayed, and still the wearisome succession of convoys continued to march along that dreary track to the zaribas. It was no use collecting a larger supply of water out there, as it went rotten if kept in the tins more than two days. We had plenty of transport in spite of our having lost so many camels, so this could not be the cause of the delay. The Transport is always made the scapegoat in war-time, and the shield behind which to hide the faults and shortcomings of others; but in this expedition it never failed, though success was gained only by superhuman exertions and willing sacrifice on the part of those who bore the brunt of the work and received no mention.

The enemy seemed now to have drawn off
towards the mountains, as they never even attempted to molest the convoys. We supposed
that Osman was concentrating at Tamai, and in
fact we heard he had strongly entrenched his
position there, and fortified it with many rifle
pits, so we looked forward to a real set-to this
time. Our hopes were therefore somewhat
damped by a story that one of our spies had
come in and reported that Osman Digna had
only about two hundred followers at Tamai, all
the remainder of his forces having dispersed to
their homes. This obtained a certain amount
of credence, from white flags having been seen
flying both towards Tamai and in the Hasheen
direction. One of these flags proved to be a
party of the enemy burying their dead of Sunday
last.

A further countermanding of the advance led
to further rumours, and I fear also a certain
amount of grumbling, in camp. It was reported
that the Amarars were leaving Osman in bodies,
giving as their reason that, while they failed to
see what they had to gain by fighting against
us, being beaten every time, they could, on the
other hand, earn good wages if they went into
Suakin, by working on the railway or at the

wharfs. The result of this was that Osman
Digna threatened them with total extermination
if they severed their allegiance with the cause.
A sanguinary fight thereupon ensued between
the Amarars and the Hadendowas. How far
this was the case we were unable to judge, but
our spies assured us that Osman had been almost
deserted, and had retired from Tamai in the
direction of Tamanieb.

On the 31st of March (Tuesday), the Mounted
Infantry and the Bengal Cavalry were sent out
to the zaribas in the afternoon, ready to reconnoitre towards Tamai on the following day.
Another small body of cavalry was despatched
in the Hasheen direction, and returned in the
evening, having seen nothing of the enemy.

Early in the morning of Wednesday, a party
of cavalry and mounted infantry marched from
the zaribas in the direction of Tamai. Having
advanced a distance of five miles or more, they
discovered that the report of the spies, that the
enemy had quitted Tamai and fallen back, was
not the case at all, and that they were still occupying that place in great force. This news, on
their return, was received with the utmost satisfaction, and it was immediately heliographed to
the camp.

Orders were issued that night that the whole of the troops, with the exception of one battalion of native infantry, were to parade the following morning at three o'clock, and that three days' provisions and as much water as possible were to be taken out with the force.

It is needless to say with what joy we received this order after the past few days of inaction, and how hard we worked that night, getting things ready for the general advance and the big fight we hoped would shortly follow. At four a.m. we were all on the move, traversing the now well-worn track to the zaribas. We moved very slowly, owing to the numbers of animals accompanying the force. The formation adopted was, as usual, a large square; but we saw nothing of the enemy, and by nine a.m. had reached the zaribas in safety.

After a rest of about an hour and a half, a further advance of five miles was made in the direction of Tamai. It was very hard work, as every man carried two days' rations, besides a full allowance of ammunition. The bush was thick and thorny, and the sun broiling. A few men fell out from exhaustion, but these came to after a drink of water, as every one was too eager about the coming fight to think of the heat, or the weight of the load, or anything else.

The balloon had been inflated at the zaribas, and accompanied the force, but the day was all against ballooning, as there was a strong wind blowing, which threatened to swing the occupant of the car out of the thing altogether. A few groups of Arabs were reported as being visible, but at length it was thought better to haul the balloon down. This was accordingly done, though not without getting it badly torn in the thorny bushes around us.

Our halting-place was not reached till well on in the afternoon, when we at once began to build a zariba. From the hill near us, known as Teselah Hill, a view of Tamai, now only two miles off, could be obtained. The eminences round us were at once occupied by half-battalions of various regiments, and a gun or two was also got into position. The ground was much rougher than that surrounding the zaribas, and further on we could see that it was covered with large rocks and boulders. From where we were a few of the enemy could be seen along the opposite ridges, but they did not attempt to interfere with us at all.

While we were thus hard at work making our

position secure for the night, the Mounted Infantry were sent forward to reconnoitre the
country between us and Tamai. Proceeding
cautiously along, they at length reached the
village without opposition, though parties of
Arabs were seen watching them at a distance.
While they were engaged looking about them
and inspecting Tamai, a brisk fire was suddenly
opened on them from some rough ground in
front, and this for the moment rather discon-
certed the men ; but a general survey of the hill
was made, and some of the huts inspected, after
which our force withdrew, having achieved all
they had been sent out to do.

It was thought by some that a night attack
would be made upon us, and all precautions
were therefore taken to avoid a surprise.

Soon after dark a somewhat heavy fire was
opened by a body of the enemy, and this continued for a while, till at one a.m. the Grenadiers,
who were out forming part of the advanced
pickets, answered with a volley or two, and the
gunners sent a few shells at them. This very
soon silenced their fire, and the remainder of
the night was passed in peace. Why the enemy
hit so few of us is very wonderful, for even
allowing for inaccuracy of aim, the mark we

R

presented to them, packed, as we were, like sardines in a tin, ought to have insured their doing a certain amount of execution.

Our casualties during the night were only one man killed and two men wounded.

The next morning, at an early hour, preparations were commenced for a further advance, and the Guards, Marines, 49th, Australians, and Sikhs were formed up ready to march on Tamai.

At eight o'clock we were on the move, formed in three sides of a square, with the Mounted Infantry and cavalry scouting in front. A few scattered parties of the enemy were seen, and these fired at us at long range. They kept themselves wonderfully under cover, and it was almost impossible for us to hit them as they retired dodging from one big stone to another.

Tamai village was eventually reached without our being attacked or seeing anything further of the enemy. The village was only quite a small place, built on a flat piece of ground standing rather above the surrounding country. It consisted entirely of huts, and there were no stone buildings of any sort. There had evidently been large flocks of sheep and many cattle there recently, and, like Hasheen village, the place had been left in a great hurry, as many of the huts were in the greatest confusion ; drinking-vessels, bead ornaments, copies of the Koran, and odds and ends of all sorts being left about everywhere.

We did not halt at the village for any length of time, as our General was anxious to secure the wells in the hollow, or wady, on the other side.

After leaving the village, I am glad to say that for once the cumbersome square formation was relinquished, and the troops advanced as for attack. We could see the enemy were in tolerable force on the opposite hills, and as we approached nearer they opened fire on us, though always keeping themselves well under cover. It was almost impossible for our skir-mishers to touch them. One of these fellows had established himself behind a big rock, and quietly fired shot after shot with a certain amount of accuracy in his aim. An officer, I think belonging to the Coldstream Guards, happened to have with him a Winchester re-peating rifle, and, putting his sight to a thousand yards, he took a steady aim, and in another second we saw the intrepid Arab who had been annoying us knocked head over heels.

Our disappointment may be imagined when,

on reaching the springs or wells, we found, instead of the running stream we had been told
to expect, only a well or two which had evidently been recently filled in by the enemy.
The engineers were set to work to dig out the
wells, while a portion of the force was sent
forward to drive the enemy from their position
on the hills. This was easily effected by the
Marines and the 49th.

All the water found was of a dark brown
colour, utterly unfit for human consumption,
and insufficient to water even a few animals.
This was a grievous disappointment to all of us,
as I, for one, had been told by a friend who was
at Suakin all through the winter months that
he had often seen through a good glass a stream
of water running down this same wady and
sparkling in the rays of the sun. That there
is a running stream here at one time of the
year is beyond a doubt true; but what we
found in the month of April was a different
thing altogether, being merely a few small wells
holding little water, and a small stagnant pool
of putrid liquid which could hardly be called
water at all.

While the Marines and the 49th were driving
the enemy back in one part of the field, the

remainder of the force were engaged dislodging them in another ; but there was no real fighting, and the enemy never showed up in force all day.

It now became evident that Osman had determined not to face us, and that he had retired towards Tamanieb, seven or eight miles further south. It was very disappointing, after all the work we had had ; but whether or not the enemy tried to draw us on, or that they had come to the wise determination of harassing us by carrying on a guerilla style of warfare, I do not know ; we had certainly come all that way for no purpose, and there was nothing for it but to return home again.

On our way back to Teselah Hill we set fire to Tamai, which was thus very soon burnt to the ground. A few rather interesting things were taken from Osman Digna's hut there, and amongst others a hand-illuminated copy of the Koran, done on separate sheets of a thick paper, and held together in a rough sort of portfolio.

It would have been quite impossible for us to hold Tamai in the face of the utter inadequacy of the water supply, and it was therefore decided to return forthwith to the zaribas.

Our losses during the day, not including the casualties of the preceding night, were, altogether, one man killed, and one officer and nine men wounded.

It was a very tedious and hot march back again that afternoon to the zaribas, where we found the 28th Native Infantry had not been molested in our absence. We left Teselah Hill about two o'clock, and did not reach the zaribas till after six p.m. There were a few cases of exhaustion from the heat, and some of the men, as soldiers always will, had drunk all their water at starting. I saw this happen over and over again during the campaign, and no amount of experience ever seemed to teach them better. We always found it best to put off drinking water as long as possible, never touching it until it was absolutely necessary, as when once we had moistened our lips the craving for more was almost irresistible. The cavalry continued their march into camp, but the remainder of the force bivouacked that night at the zaribas.

I have never devoted any remarks to the Mounted Infantry. A hardier and more willing lot of fellows it would be difficult to find anywhere; they were always to the front, and you would see them galloping about in the bush or clattering up the hills on their little Arab horses, who suited them down to the ground, and were just the animals for the job. There is one thing, though, which I think calls for a remark, and that is the manner in which the Mounted Infantry were utilized during the campaign. Every Mounted Infantry man is armed only with a rifle, and he carries his ammunition on a cross-belt, bandoleer fashion. It is a recognized thing with them that they are not to engage the enemy under four hundred yards, unless driven to do so by circumstances, their duties being to harass the enemy at a distance by the accuracy of their fire, and to move rapidly from point to point. They were, however, in the Sûdan continually used as cavalry, which, there is no doubt about it, was a grave mistake. They are utterly unsuited for the work for several reasons, but principally because, in the event of their being attacked by cavalry when mounted, they are practically unarmed, as they carry no swords. It is no doubt a great difficulty to know how to separate the two organizations of Mounted Infantry and cavalry, and to keep each intact in its own individuality. If you give a Mounted Infantry man a sword you practically make a cavalry man of him, as both then are armed

almost identically. To keep Mounted Infantry
as a distinct force, and to separate them entirely
from the cavalry, the only way is never to use
them for duties for which they are unsuited.
When the cavalry is hardly worked, there is a
great likelihood of the Mounted Infantry being
taken for outpost duty, and the ordinary routine
of vidette work ; but for these duties they are
unsuited, and, moreover, were never intended.
In our next big war I conceive that Mounted
Infantry will play, to a certain extent, an important part. The force is only still in its
infancy, and now is the time that arrangements
should be made to give it a distinct place of its
own in the army, and not make it up, on the
spur of the moment, of units from various regiments, and then in the field require it to perform
duties for which it is utterly unfitted, and for the
performance of which we have already an organ-
ized force in our cavalry. To fire and scuttle
away, and never to engage the enemy at close
quarters, should be the two rules for the guidance
alike of Mounted Infantry men themselves, and
those who utilize them.

After the two exceedingly severe days' work
entailed upon the troops by the advance on
Tamai, every one slept pretty soundly in the

zaribas that night, and nothing took place to disturb us.

The next morning the whole force, with the exception of the 28th Native Infantry, who were left behind to look after the zaribas till the stores there could be withdrawn, marched back to their old quarters in front of Suakin.

The enormous concourse of men and animals may be imagined when I say that, besides a fighting force of 8175 men, there were also 752 camels, over 1000 mules, 1773 drivers and followers, eight ambulance waggons, a number of mule-carts, a great many dhoolies, and two field-hospitals, together with seventeen wounded and thirty-three sick.

When one considers what it means to feed such a force as this, and provide water every day for nearly 12,000 throats, miles from the base, and in a country where there is nothing but dried-up bush and parching sands, the work, to say the least of it, seems a heavy one.

All our toil and labour in collecting supplies at the zaribas had now gone for nothing. I do not know what the General thought, but many of us likened ourselves, on our return to camp that day, to the soldiers of a certain king of France, who amused himself marching much such an army as we were, in point of strength, to the top of a hill and down again.

The day after we got back to camp was Easter Sunday, and we were allowed a day of comparative rest.

On the following morning, at 4.30, an enormous convoy of baggage animals, numbering over two thousand camels and fifteen hundred mules, escorted by four battalions of infantry, marched out for the last time to the zaribas, to bring in all the stores and the garrison, and to a certain extent to destroy the place. With the exception of a few trusses of hay everything was brought in, the convoy returning to camp shortly before six o'clock in the evening. The 28th Native Infantry had been fired at for nearly three hours the previous night, but only one man and two mules were wounded. The mere fact of the enemy having dared to follow us on our retreat from Tamai, and to open fire again on the zaribas, shows how little real moral effect our operations had had upon them.

Thus ended our connection with those three zaribas, dyed so indelibly with the blood of so many brave men on both sides.

The campaign thus far seemed barren of results indeed. How far any plan was carried out by these marches here and marches there, I know not; but many able men thought it would have been much better had we made the line of the railway the line of our advance, and avoided the loss of life and excessive toil entailed by marching after Osman Digna wherever he chose to lead us. Had we acted in this way, Osman would have been bound to attack us, or lost for ever his prestige with his followers. He would have fought then at a disadvantage to himself, and with a corresponding advantage to us; and we should have been able to devote our energies the whole while towards pushing on the railway, which was, after all, one of the principal objects of the expedition. Many men who had spent years of their life in the country, travelling about and studying the character of the natives, were of opinion, even before we landed at Suakin, that this latter course would have been the one adopted by our leaders. But here we were, after many weeks spent in marching about the country, back again at our starting-point, doing exactly what it was supposed we should do, even before the troops left England.

It appeared evident that, as far as fighting was concerned, the campaign might now be considered over, and that we need not expect any serious opposition from Osman Digna.

Our spies also informed us that Osman had been almost entirely deserted by most of the tribes, and had retired with a few hundred followers to a point between Sinkat and Erkowit.

While the stores were being withdrawn from the zaribas, the remainder of the troops were busily engaged concentrating the whole of the camp along the line of railway, which had now reached as far as the West Redoubt, a distance of nearly four miles from Suakin.

A force, consisting of the Coldstream Guards, the Australian battalion, 17th Company Royal Engineers, two guns of the Mule Battery, and a troop of cavalry, marched, early the same morning, five miles out in the direction of Handoub, where a zariba was formed. This zariba was known as No. 1 zariba, and was constructed partially to protect the line of railway, and also as a halting-place and depôt midway between the West Redoubt and Handoub, which place was to be our next object.

The enemy had actually begun to renew their night attacks on the camp, and, the first night we returned, a party attempted to rush the Marines, but were discovered and fired upon before they could do any damage. How little they had profited by the severe chastisement they had at all times received may be judged of from this fact.

The force at No. 1 zariba moved forward the morning after their arrival there, their place being taken by the Scots Guards, with a large convoy of stores and provisions.

It was not expected that the enemy would offer any serious opposition to our advance on Handoub, but every precaution was taken, as the bush at the foot of the hills is remarkably thick. The Mounted Infantry scouted the ground in front, but only a few Arabs were seen watching our movements from a distance.

It was a terribly hot morning, and the men suffered very much on this tedious march through the heavy sand. Handoub was at length reached, and occupied without any opposition at all. The place, which consisted only of a few huts, was entirely deserted. The wells, altogether five in number, were found to contain a fair supply of somewhat brackish water. One of the five gave a rather better quality than the others, but a plentiful supply of drinkable water was obtained by digging in the bed of the khor. It was not, of course, free from the brackish taste, but a little citric acid mixed with it over-

came this.   Water was sent out to Handoub by
the convoys, in the same way as we had been
doing before ; but we hoped that, as soon as the
railway reached there, this part of our labours
would be over.   All along the side of the line
four-inch pipes had been laid to carry water to
the front, and patent pumps had been sent out
to force it any distance.

Handoub is the first halting-place on the
traders' route from Suakin to Berber, and is
situated at the foot of a low isolated ridge or
spur of the Waratab Mountains, which here run
down into the plain.   It is twelve and a half
miles north-west of Suakin.

After an interval for rest after the hot march,
a zariba was commenced between two small
hills which commanded the village, and a gun
was also mounted on the top of each hill, so the
position was as secure as it well could be, and,
with the Australians and Coldstreams to defend
it, could have held out against any numbers.

The following day a large convoy was sent out
to Handoub, escorted by a squadron of cavalry ;
the remainder of the troops being engaged in
cutting "drifts" and making a broad track in
the bush for the railway.

This drift-making was terribly hard work in

the burning sun, as the wood of the mimosa and acacia is very tough indeed, and it is almost impossible to get at the stems of these stunted bushes, owing to the thorns. The way our men managed it was to sling a rope round a bush, and then, while two men hauled on the rope to pull the branches on one side, a third would attack the stem with an axe. When the bush was cut down it had to be dragged out of the way by more men ; so the work was altogether very slow and very hard.

I think the most tedious work of all was guarding the head of the railway. A force of cavalry and infantry was told off for this duty each day, and while some of the men were placed on sentry, the rest were allowed to lie down on the ground, ready at any moment in the event of an attack. A few tent roofs were sent out, to protect the men from the sun ; but as these were insufficient in number, many of the men would lie down on the sand, and go fast to sleep in the full blaze of the sun. With nothing to occupy them and little to think about all day long, the men had nothing left to do but to go to sleep. A guard of this sort was absolutely necessary to cover the working parties, but the Arabs never interfered with us, and so there was not even the excitement of a little skirmish to while away the time. I really believe some of the men would rather have been engaged on the railway fatigue, or in cutting the "drifts," than as covering party to the workers.

There was rather an amusing story told of one of the navvies at this time. The line had very nearly reached No. 1 zariba, and of course there was a large quantity of sleepers, fish-plates, rails, etc., collected in front, to be used up as the railway proceeded. One morning a navvy happened to go out rather earlier than usual, and found an Arab asleep among the sleepers. While he was debating in his mind what he should do with the fellow, the Arab suddenly woke up, and in the twinkling of an eye sent his spear flying at the somewhat astonished navvy. Stepping gracefully on one side, the navvy is said to have caught the spear as it passed him. Walking up then to the Arab, without more ado he planted a blow, with his clenched fist and in true English fashion, right between the fellow's eyes, which knocked him about ten yards into the bush. Having settled him in this way, the navvy walked up to his prostrate and insensible foe, and brought him in a prisoner.

One of our Indian drivers who had been missing ever since our fight at Hasheen, turned up in camp in the middle of this week, having been a prisoner all the while in the hands of Osman Digna. His story was that, when he was about to be killed by some of the Hadendowas, he declared himself a Mohammedan, and this saved his life. He was taken to Tamai, and after the fight at the zaribas, the Arabs returned there with seven more of our native drivers, who had been cut off in their flight to Suakin. He had had an interview with Osman Digna, who, he said, had given orders that Mohammedan prisoners were to be treated with kindness. He also said that, although on the day we visited Tamai there were only a few men there, there was a large force further on in the mountains, but that they were all badly off for food.

The 2nd Brigade was moved further up the line as the rest of the force advanced, and pitched their camp about two miles from the No. 1 zariba, in readiness for a further advance when required.

We were daily engaged running convoys out to Handoub, and occasionally we had for our escort only a small body of cavalry. This did not seem altogether a wise measure, considering

S

the lesson we had already learnt from treating the enemy with too much indifference. On one occasion our friends in No. 1 zariba watched us, expecting every moment to see us attacked, as a few hundred Arabs were seen on the hills quite close to our line of march. It was a curious thing, that, although we never knew exactly where the enemy might be, our returning convoys not unfrequently moved without an escort at all. Another serious loss in camels would have crippled our transport very considerably, but still these risks were run, and the safety of our camels left to chance.

In our advance to Handoub, we were accompanied by Mahomet Ali, the friendly sheikh of the Amarar tribe, who had been endeavouring to persuade the Amarars to come in in a body, though not with much success. After the short campaign last year the "friendlies" had suffered severely at the hands of Osman Digna, as soon as we had sailed away in our ships, and they were naturally not altogether inclined to run the chance of the same thing occurring again. They therefore demanded that we should guarantee their protection before they submitted. This it was impossible to grant, as we had no idea what the future policy of the Government might be with relation to the Sûdan.

On the 13th of April the Mounted Infantry reconnoitred the country as far as Otao without meeting with any of the enemy. Two wells were found containing a small amount of water, and it appeared probable that more might be obtained by digging. The ground all the way from Handoub to Otao, a distance of five miles, is more open, the bush being much less thick. On the 16th Otao was occupied by the Scots Guards, with two guns and a squadron of the 5th Lancers. Nothing was seen of the enemy.

There was a good deal of sickness now among the troops, principally from dysentery and sun-troke, but enteric fever was also increasing, and one or two cases had terminated fatally. The work was very hard, as it always must be in war-time, the weather was frightfully hot, and the climate not of the best, so what with the want of good food and water and the incessant labour from dawn till dark, the percentage of sick was slowly rising, and the hospitals were filling apace.

The campaign dragged slowly on, and there was no fighting to relieve the drudgery of the day, the long marches, or the never-ending con-voys. A good fight would have brightened us all up, but it was evident now that Osman Digna did not intend to try issues with us again. We heard he was doing his utmost to collect his followers, but the tribes were all engaged up in the mountains sowing their crops. A few scattered bands still hovered about the country, but these generally made off when any of our cavalry or Mounted Infantry approached, and the whole country appeared deserted.

The most extraordinary rumours reached us from England, about the Government being pressed to withdraw from the Sûdan altogether, and give up the destruction of the tribes, against whom we had no real quarrel. We hardly credited this, though, and we could not believe that the enormous outlay and loss of life would have been allowed unless the Government had had some decided aim in view.

Berber seemed a very long way off to us, and we still had two hundred and sixty miles left to do. I do not think we ever imagined for a moment that the railway would be carried all the way, and with the hot season now beginning we thought we had quite enough before us to get to Ariab, before the autumn. How much of the force would eventually reach Berber in time for the advance on Khartoum was a matter of the vaguest speculation, the general idea being that we should not participate at all in this part of the programme, but merely occupy a point to threaten the enemy's flank and cut off their retreat in this direction when Khartoum had fallen.   So, as I say, the days and hours dragged on, the hospitals filled, the sick were sent away homeward, and those that were left toiled on in their now ragged clothes from sunrise till sunset.

CHAPTER XI.

HOSPITAL.

A DHOOLIE is a comfortable conveyance. I was
carried some miles in one. I was to have been
sent down to hospital in a cart drawn by a pair
of mules, till some one suggested this would be
a painful experience. So a dhoolie was sent for,
and shortly after I was lying inside it, with my
water-bottle for a pillow and my small amount
of kit following behind on a camel.

Let me explain what a dhoolie is to those
who have never seen one. Suspended from a
thick bamboo pole some ten feet in length is
a light iron frame six feet six inches long and
three feet broad. Across this frame is stretched
some stout canvas, while at the ends and sides
a similar piece of material, about six inches
broad, is fixed round to prevent the occupant
from falling out. The corners of the iron framework are fitted with short legs, so that when the

dhoolie is put down the person inside does not touch the ground. Curtains, two feet six inches high, go all round the dhoolie, fitted at the top to a cane framework, the roof being made of a swinging sort of awning of thick canvas. The bearers are eight in number, and two work at a time at each end of the pole ; so there are two reliefs, and no stoppage need be made. These dhoolie-bearers are Indians regularly trained in the art of carrying the sick. They move at a sort of running shuffle, taking care to break the step so as to stop any swinging of the dhoolie. The sort of shuffling noise these fellows make with their feet will, no doubt, recall many sad experiences, and maybe also hours of much suffering, to those who have been carried in a dhoolie in war-time.

"Good-bye, old chap," from a friend, and "*challow* Quarantine Island" (go on to Quarantine Island) to the bearers, and I was on my journey to one of the hospital-ships in the harbour.

I do not know how far I had gone when the dhoolie was quietly put on the ground, and I heard the bearers sit themselves down and begin talking.

Theirs happened to be one of the many

languages I was unable to talk, and, moreover, I was too ill to raise my voice much above a whisper; but, pulling aside one of the curtains, I saw I was near some tents, and as there was a sergeant standing by, I made signs to him to come to me. The only answer I received from this individual was, "You bide where you are;" so no doubt he did not recognize me as an officer —how should he in the rags I had on?

At length I managed, by pointing to my bearers the direction in which I wished to go, to start them again, and nothing particular occurred for the next mile save the periodical changing of the reliefs.

After a while I was again put on the ground, and this time found myself at the Base Hospital at " H " Redoubt.

"What have you got here?" says a sentry to the bearers—the English soldier always thinks every one must speak his language. "Oh, a officer, is it? Well, what's the use a-bringing on 'im 'ere? I tell ye he's for Quarantine Island."

But by this time a doctor had come up, who very kindly asked me whether I should like to go on by train, as the " Flying Hadendowa " would be passing directly. Thinking that the dhoolie would be more comfortable than the somewhat primitive Suakin-Berber railway, I said that on the whole I would rather stick to my dhoolie. Thus I lost my chance of a ride on this famous line, which some one naïvely described as a line which begins nowhere and ends nowhere else.

This time I really did get to Quarantine Island ; and when my bearers stopped again another doctor pulled my curtains aside, and, shaking me by the hand, said, " You will have to wait a bit, but we will have a boat for you presently ; meanwhile we will draw these curtains aside, and you will get the air." So I lay like this for half an hour, surrounded by all the bustle and the dust of that busy landing-place. Many came and stared at me, and passed remarks the reverse of inspiriting.

" Well, he's a gone coon, anyhow," said one. " Lor', don't he look ill ! " said another. " Sunstroke," said a third. " I tell ye he isn't sunstroke," said a fourth ; " 'e've been wounded," and so on. They settled it between them somehow or other, but how made little difference to me.

The boat came at last, and then, being unable to move, I was rolled out of the dhoolie into

the dust, and picked up and put in the boat.
Ten minutes' pulling brought me to the hospital-
ship. I was carried up the side, and in another
minute found myself on a comfortable bed in a
cabin all to myself, too ill to care much about
anything, and too tired to do anything but fall
asleep at once. I shall never forget the peace,
quiet, and contentment of the first few hours in
that small cabin. The air blew in cool through
the port, the silence was only broken by the
plashing of the water against the ship's great
sides, and with this music in my ears I fell
asleep.

They were very kind to us in hospital, and
everything that could be done was done for the
sick and the wounded. It seemed very odd to
hear a woman's voice again, and we ought all to
be very grateful for the loving care bestowed
upon us by the lady nurses. There were many
of these, both in the shore-hospitals as well as in
the two hospital-ships, and their scarlet capes ·
and cheery faces did much to brighten up the
different tents and cabins. We often talk of the
way we soldiers are ordered off here and there
at short notice, but I think few soldiers ever
started for foreign service with shorter notice
than did some of these lady nurses. I knew of

one, aged not more than one and twenty, who
received her orders for Suakin at nine o'clock
one night and had to be ready to sail the next
morning at seven. What can we say of such
devotion as this, of a readiness to share with the
soldiers their trials and hardships, to tend them
when sick, and to soothe them in their hours of
greatest suffering? To brave all the horrors of
a military hospital, and to fight at the same time
against a climate, requires a noble spirit indeed,
and women who are able and willing to undertake such duties, forgetful of self, and mindful
only of the sufferings of others, should rank
among the very highest of their sex. Women
teach us many things, but above all they teach
us unselfishness.

One of the greatest drawbacks to our hospital
was the enormous number of rats. I awoke
one night to find upwards of a dozen in my
cabin. They were the most confidential rats
I ever saw, and they seemed to know perfectly well that, being a cripple, I was unable
to get at them. They would take a jump right
across from the bunk on one side of the cabin
on to the top of me; but I got accustomed to
them at last, and quite content that they should
enjoy themselves so long as they did not crawl

over my face. Besides the rats, there were thousands and thousands of cockroaches of all sizes, the largest measuring an inch and a half long.   Some people would have objected to these more than the rats, but I preferred anything to the cold paws of a rat on my face. That was really objectionable, and, what was worse, it generally woke one up with a start.

There were cases of all sorts in hospital— wounds of the most curious and interesting description, the doctors said ; cases of sunstroke, many of dysentery, fevers of various kinds, affections of the eyes, small-pox, and even cholera.   The small-pox patients were kept on · a lighter at the entrance to the harbour, and I never heard of more than two cases of cholera.

I think the one I pitied more than most was an officer who had served his country in the Crimea and in China, and who had had a lengthened experience in the Sûdan besides.   A finer soldier and a kinder-hearted or more genial man I never met.   He was suffering from an acute attack of some disease of the eyes which rendered him for the time blind.   Being, of course, unable to read, and having nothing to occupy himself with, he used to wander up and down the saloon all day long, and when night came he was unable to sleep for pain. One day a ship started for home with invalids and he was ordered in her, but at the last moment they had no room for him, and he was condemned to another week or more on the hospital-ship. He never murmured, he was always cheerful; but when the ship came at last and took him away, he reached England but to die.

There were many cases as sad as this, and many died ere reaching home—victims to a climate and to the hardships of war. Denied the glory of a death in the heat of action, they succumbed to the foe that slays in greater numbers than either the spear or the bullet—a death less glorious, perhaps, but a life given for Queen and Country just the same. The sorrows following after a war are, for the most part, localized. The nation feels not as a whole the loss of its soldiers; but they feel who find gaps where formerly stood cheery, manly forms, who miss the ring of the voice they loved so well, and the light heart and ready grip of the hand. The day will come when the troops will return, the towns will be gay with many-coloured flags, bands will play and crowds will cheer, and who among all the concourse that watch that home-coming will miss the forms of those who come not?

Our friends came to see us in hospital when time would allow, but many were too far up the country now to come down easily to Suakin. Let me give one instance of the way one soldier helps another. I was lying on my bed one hot afternoon, the temperature even in the cool of the hospital being 88° all through the day, when in comes a friend, saying, " Here are your letters, old chap. Good-bye ; I can't stop."

That friend had ridden many miles in all the fierce heat of a noonday sun, and when over-done with work, to bring me what soldiers value most on service—home news.

May I thank him here ?

And now my story is almost over. One night they told me they were going to send me home. I don't know that the news was good news, for I would far rather have come home with the rest ; and though the war was said to be over, I did not like leaving friends behind.

The next morning, early, we were put on board a lighter and towed off to the ship that was to take us home.

We were put on board with our baggage, and stood for some time on the lower deck waiting for our cabins to be told off to us. We were a motley-looking crowd certainly as we stood or sat there in our ragged, worn-out clothes. There were a good many of us. Men with bandaged heads, with arms in slings, with battered helmets and torn jackets. Men looking ill and worn, and with that peculiar expression of countenance begotten of days of fatigue, of nights of anxious watching, of hours of suffering, and times of great privation.

Why does not one of our great artists paint a picture such as this ? The world would rave about it, people would stand by the hour and gaze at it, crowds would wonder at it, and women would weep over it, while some might faintly realize the sufferings of the men who are content to go out with a smile upon their countenances, to brave hourly, daily, nightly, death in its most horrible forms, and then to return, some of them, a shadow of their former selves.

" Soldiers," said one of England's greatest generals, " your labours, your privations, your sufferings, and your valour will not be forgotten by a grateful country."

We pray this may be so.

THE END.

PRINTED BY WILLIAM CLOWES AND SONS, LIMITED,
LONDON AND BECCLES.